To Kai
Daddy's child a
good one and, with
the grace of God it
saw us through.
Mildred Dennis

IT'S GONNA BE OK

A Lease-Child's Legacy

by

Mildred Dennis

authorHOUSE™

1663 LIBERTY DRIVE, SUITE 200
BLOOMINGTON, INDIANA 47403
(800) 839-8640
WWW.AUTHORHOUSE.COM

First published by AuthorHouse 10/08/04

ISBN: 1-4208-0306-9 (e)
ISBN: 1-4208-0305-0 (sc)

Library of Congress Control Number: 2004097550

Printed in the United States of America
Bloomington, Indiana

This book is printed on acid-free paper.

Cover Photos by Donna Skufca

Shotgun House *from Sinclair Plant 12*
Displayed on grounds of The Oklahoma Oil Museum and Seminole Historical Society
Seminole, OK

With Grateful Thanks To

Mama and Daddy

And the Good Lord who let me grow up with the blessings of living my life of freedom as a Lease Child

PART ONE

UP ON THE HILL

"Oh hum-hum-hum!"

The deep sigh could be heard several seats away, but the weary passengers looked at the little girl with understanding eyes. It had been a long, long night on the Missouri part of the Mother Road. The bus groaned up one graveled mountain, bounced down another, then crawled around the hairpin turns. It would be a few more years before any kind of permanent road would be laid down on Route 66.

She wiggled around on the hard seat till she was on her knees. By stretching, she could see the sunrise as it began to highlight the brilliant reds and golds trembling in the haze which often creeps across the tops of the Ozarks in late September.

"Mama, are we almost there?"

"Not yet. Just go to sleep." The mother patted the little girl; then closed her own weary eyes.

The little girl wondered, "How can Mama sleep. She's missing all this good stuff to see." That drugstore bus stop in central Illinois seemed far, far away. Trees reached for the sky on all sides; long rickety bridges crossed over tumbling rivers. The little girl wished she could read the signs at the sides of the road. Sometimes the bus pulled into a town and stopped; and the driver would call out as he opened the door, "Waynesville (or some other name), ten minutes."

As the passengers rushed for the door, the mama would push the little girl ahead. "Hurry, we don't have much time." After taking care of business, it was back on the bus.

At last, it was afternoon again. The bus was passing a few more buildings. "This must be another town." But it wasn't just another town, it was "the town." The driver pulled up in front of a stone building, called out, "Seminole, Oklahoma, thirty minutes." and opened the door.

This was the stop she had been waiting for. The little girl looked out the window, and there he stood, smiling all over his face. "Daddy!"

She slipped out of the seat, ran down the aisle and jumped down the steps into his waiting arms. After a hug for Mama, he swept her up again and laughed, "Let's go home."

I was the four-year-old who had made that long bus ride; the year was 1933, and my Oklahoma lease-life experience was just beginning.

Daddy picked up our suitcase, we climbed into the old Model A Ford and headed out of town. Almost immediately, I saw something new, something I'd never seen before. "Daddy, look at all those funny windmills."

"Nah, those aren't windmills, they're oil derricks." Daddy explained. "They're the reason we're down here. They pump the oil. The ones that look like Christmas trees with lights running to the top are being drilled. About 25 years ago there wasn't much of anything around here except the Indians. Now most of Seminole County and some of Pottawatomie County are filled with these oil wells and people have moved in from all over the country. You know, Thelm', there are a lot of people here from Illinois."

The idea of oil exploration of the east central Oklahoma pools began as a dream of a shoe salesman named O.D. Strother. After seeing a geological survey map made by the U.S. Government, he became convinced there was oil flowing deep beneath the red dirt. Strother moved to Tidmore, OK, which became Seminole in 1905, and began to buy leases. For $5 an acre, he bought the 80 acres southeast of Seminole on which Sinclair Plant 12 was later built.

Strother started drilling wells, but <u>all</u> were dry holes. Unfortunately, the dreamer died in 1926 with his dream still out there, never to know how close he came. Less than a year after his death, companies began drilling to deeper sands and found rivers of oil flowing deep under the red dirt. Strother's land-poor estate reached about $7,000,000. He hasn't been forgotten; one of the main streets in Seminole bears his name.

By the time Daddy drove into town in 1933, Seminole had earned the reputation of being the toughest boomtown in America. I heard him telling Mama that he almost didn't stay because one of the first sights he saw was a shooting. It seemed a silly argument. Which one of two guys would be first to walk the narrow board that crossed over the mud to the other side of Main Street? As it turned out, neither one crossed over. The guy shot lay face down in the mud; the shooter was held till a policeman came.

All I know is that it didn't take long for me to feel right at home with the oil wells and each night the rhythm of the engines became a lullaby "singing" me to sleep. (Years later, on the East Central College campus in Ada, I missed the sound of those engines lullabies. It was too quiet, and for awhile sleep was slow to come.)

About four miles from town, our old car climbed a rutted, red dirt hill and stopped at the top. "This is it," said Daddy. "It" was a three-room, unpainted shotgun house in a row of about five or six other boomshacks. Mama looked none too happy.

We found very little furniture inside, but there was a new bed for me. Actually it was a big old metal baby crib, but that was O.K. by me—it was mine.

There were some things that Mama DID like—water gushed from a pipe when she turned the handle (no more wells and pitcher pumps). Electric lights came on like magic when I pulled the string. No more oil lamps spreading scary goblin shadows into the corners. No more cooking with wood—that was replaced with the yellow-tipped blue flame of gas. Of course this was a mixed blessing; we ate our way through many plates of burned food before Mama learned that it was quite O.K. to turn the gas flame a little lower before the pan burned black.

For the twenty years that we lived on the company leases, all residents shared the pluses of gas, water, and electricity.

Why had we made this long journey from my uncle's tiny truck farm in central Illinois to a God-forsaken (my mama's words) Sinclair oil lease in the middle of nowhere? "Besides," quoted Mama, "everyone knows there are wild Indians all around here," and for awhile, Mama was deathly afraid of all those "wild" Indians. But, it was 1933, the height of the depression and Daddy needed a job badly; so like it or not, we were here to stay.

When Mama's cousin, the superintendent of Sinclair Plant 12 near Seminole, had contacted Daddy in Illinois, the message read, "We need roustabouts out here in the oilfields. Would you and Thelma be willing to move to Oklahoma?" There was the key, would Mama be willing to move? She'd already persuaded Daddy to leave one job so she could go home, and that was only over in Indiana. Well, of course, Mama wasn't willing and she resisted with all her might; but Daddy told Fred Pearce that he would come as soon as possible. And so it was that I became a "lease child."

The first hot morning in my new home seemed like summer to me. I couldn't wait to get outside. At first, shyness kept me close to the house, but before lunchtime, my natural curiosity took over. In the row of houses, the Gilkey family lived on one side of us and the Dixon family on the other, both with kids about my age, Joan and Don. The Dunagans "company" house was just around the corner. This meant their house was bigger and nicer than most, had a coat of paint and a full-sized front porch.

(Small world note.) Many years later when I moved to Arcola, Illinois, imagine my surprise to find "little" Georgie Dunagan living right across the street. The first thing George and I did was pick up the on-going dispute about who really had won the contests for jumping the greatest distance off the porch railings so long ago. The contests would go on and on till George's mom would come out and shoo us all home. "Somebody's gonna break a leg for sure!" Luckily no one ever did.

Don Dixon's Grandma and Grandpa Thompson lived in an even smaller house at the end of the row. They were "really old" and became my very first Indian friends. At least I think Grandpa Thompson was a friend. He usually sat in his chair under a giant Cottonwood tree, puffed on his pipe and watched us play. I guess he could talk but I never actually heard him say a word. Don claimed that sometimes Grandpa could tell the best stories about the old days in Indian Territory, but only when no one else was around.

It was different with Grandma Thompson. She talked a lot—not that I could always understand what she was saying. But I sure could understand when she called us for Fry Bread, which she shared generously with all the kids. It came straight from the fry pan and burned our fingers and blistered our tongues as we gulped it down. Today I would compare that

7

brown crispy goodness with the Israelites' "manna from heaven." During the time I was teaching at Centerview (near Prague), Mama Rice, my Sac and Fox "stand-in" Indian mama, tried to teach me to make fry bread, but I never really did get the knack of patting it out just right. The center was always too thick, so it didn't cook through to that crispy goodness. I know it was never as good as Grandma Thompson's, but once in awhile, even today, I still try.

Don and Joan and I soon became the incorrigible musketeers. Each one would try to outdo the other and this got us into trouble fairly often—especially the day we played "doctor" in the shed behind the bunk house. Too bad for me, Mama found us and I got a whippin' all the way home and had to stay in my bed the rest of the day.

"But Mama," I kept trying to explain. "Be quiet, you bad girl. Wait till your dad gets home." She promised a "real talkin' to" from Daddy, but the only thing I remember is that he let me out of bed for supper. I do know that my doctor playing days ended that day forever.

Everybody liked to play "Tornado Comin." We spent hours carrying water and building rows and rows of houses and streets in the sandy place by the side of the road. Grandpa Thompson's Cottonwood tree shaded it most of the day. It was perfect. To build a good house, we packed the damp sand over a bare foot; then carefully slipped the foot out. If the sand didn't fall in, we called it a house. After a while someone would shout, "Tornado comin! Tornado comin!" — and with stomping feet, we would flatten every single house we'd built.

We'd step back, look it over, and congratulate ourselves on a job well-done. Then we'd start the house building all over again. (It seems to me this is the Oklahoma way when the dreaded tornadoes sweep across the land—just step back, look the situation over and start rebuilding.)

There were many temptations on the lease. Every Mom warned about the slush pits. "Stay away from them. You could get lost in the oil and we'd never find you." But when the hot Oklahoma sun combined with the constant wind, the top and edges of the pit would bake into a curling, dusty Lorelei. The surface lured a kid to come on, one barefoot step at a time. It didn't help to have the other kids yelling, "I dare ya'. I double dare ya'."

I usually stood back a little ways and watched. Some brave soul would take a step or two, breaking a few curls around the edge, then back out very slowly. Not me though—I was more afraid of the storm my mama would raise than the slush pit. Finally one unlucky day for me, Joan started teasing, "Let's do it. I will if you will." She stepped on the first curling edge—nothing happened. "Come on," she said, "what's the matter, fraidy cat."

That did it. The vision of Mama's storm blew right out of my head. Slowly I put my foot forward. As the curl broke, the crackling sound sent shivers down my back. I waited! Nothing bad happened. Slowly, slowly I inched forward as the crumbling curls tickled my toes. I gritted my teeth, expecting to be swallowed up any minute. The thought passed across my mind, "Maybe I'd better get out now." But I just couldn't. I crept further and a little further, till suddenly the crust gave way. I wasn't swallowed up, but I was standing like a crane with one foot mired in the muddy oil up over my ankle.

Not only was I still expecting to disappear from sight, but "Oh my gosh!" I suddenly remembered Mama. I panicked, but the other kids shouted encouragement, including Joan, who had backed away from the pit's edge before she ever stepped beyond that first curl. Once the top was broken, I sank with every step I took while backing out, but I made it.

All the kids helped with sticks and leaves, but we couldn't scrape the oil off. Suddenly they began running in all directions. I looked around to see the reason for the desertions. It was Mama comin' at top speed, and I was left to face her all by myself. Besides the "whipping," I had to stay in my own yard for what seemed forever. Those smart-alecky kids were nice enough to wave as they walked by and call out "sweetly," "Hey, how long before you can play again?"

I've thought of that slush pit more than a few times. It had such an innocent inviting look on top, but the sticky black muck didn't want to turn me loose. Though it's not always possible, I've tried to avoid life's slush pits as often as I can.

A drilling crew had been working in the field behind our houses for quite a while. We would climb up on the fence behind Mama's garden and watch as they hauled in all kinds of equipment, dug trenches and those awful slush pits, and put up the derrick. Usually it didn't seem too much was going on; the pipes went down and the pipes came up. But one day as we climbed up on the fence, we knew somethin' was goin' on. The guys were rushing around more than usual and shouting back and forth. As we watched, a kind of a rumble began, kinda like thunder that rolls on and on. We checked the sky; just like most days, no clouds, just blue sky.

We looked at each other, then the most amazing thing happened. The ground began to shake, and there before our eyes, a fountain of black gushed up over the top of the derrick and began spraying down on the men. We thought, "Gosh, somethin' musta broke." But as we watched the guys were acting happy. They threw their hats into the air, and danced around like a bunch of crazy puppets. I know Mama wasn't real pleased when some of the oil blew over onto her struggling garden.

At supper, Daddy was excited as he said, "That well is a real gusher. This is a good thing."

Later that night I gave it some thought. I wondered how something so messy could be a good thing. I guess I should have asked Daddy about that, but my recent slush pit walk colored my thinking a little. I figured the least said about "oily messes" the better.

My favorite place to be was always anyplace outside. But occasionally, if we had a cold or rainy day, I did like to play paper dolls—the best part was cutting them out and trying to find clothes in the old Montgomery Ward's catalogues and make them fit. On a sunny day Joan and I would spread everything out under the Cottonwood tree and hope that pesky Oklahoma wind didn't come along and blow everything away.

We would show our paper creations dressed in the latest Montgomery Ward styles to Grandpa Thompson. His response would be an extra cloud of smoke rising around his head. Was he sending out smoke signals seeking some help to deal with these "crazy" girls?

Joan had a couple of dolls, but I don't remember having a doll, or even playing with hers. What I do remember is the one doll I coveted with a passion. (I guess "covet" is an adult word, but as I look back, that is the perfect word for what I felt then.)

The darling of the whole country in the mid to late '30's was Shirley Temple. With my black Dutch bob shingled up the back, there was no way I could compete with her golden curls, or those deep, deep dimples. I spent hours with my fingers stuck in my cheeks, trying to make dimples. It never happened!

Shirley Temple dolls were all the rage, but my folks were trying to pay for the new stove and refrigerator. There was no way I was gonna have a Shirley Temple doll. "Why would you want a doll anyway?" Mama would ask, then she would turn to Daddy, "You know she'd rather be outside playing in the dirt." So Shirley stayed in the store window, and I worshiped the golden curls and dimples from afar.

We heard that the Rialto Theater was giving away a few Shirley Temple dolls to some lucky winners. At the Saturday night show we got tickets to put in the big, round drum. I thought surely I would win one of those beautiful dolls..

But it wasn't to be. A friend of Mama's, Mrs. Prust, won one. That doll was a tall as me, and she always sat on Mrs. Prust's bed looking all blonde and beautiful. I couldn't understand why a grown-up lady would want that doll; surely she would want to give it to me. Of course, that didn't happen, but when Mama and I went to visit, I thought maybe she would let me hold Shirley. Well, that didn't happen either. The truth is that I saw Mrs. Prust as a fat, grouchy old lady, and I didn't like her very much.

While Mama and Mrs. Prust visited in the front room, somehow, someway, I found myself in the bedroom. There sat Shirley, smiling away. I just wanted to touch her dimples, so I very carefully (and quietly) climbed up on that bed, crawled over to the doll, and holding my breath, reached out to touch her. It was about that time that Mrs. Lony Prust waddled in with Mama right behind her.

She was screaming at the top of her voice, "Don't you dare touch my Shirley, you bad, bad girl!" She jerked me off the bed none too gently.

There was no time nor was anyone really interested in my wailing, "But I wasn't gonna hurt Shirley, I just wanted to touch her dimples."

Mama's swats were pretty half-hearted as she put me into the car. No one could miss the bang when Mrs. Prust slammed the door. I thought, "Well, that's probably the last time we'll go to that house," and I was glad.

This led to one of my unhappiest childhood memories. Unfortunately, Mrs. Prust became very sick not long after the Shirley episode and before many weeks had passed, she died. (Cancer was something to be reckoned with even then.).

This was my first glimpse of death and my understanding of what had happened was very limited. Some very "bad" thoughts about this lady had filled my mind, and I seriously wondered if it was my fault that she had died. Of course, I didn't dare tell anyone about this, not even Daddy. I understand now that there was some pretty "self-important" thinking going on in my mind, but death can leave a four-year-old with some really confused wonderings.

I'm not sure that anyone even thought about explaining things to kids then, so my guilt trip went on for a long, long time. To make it even worse, I sometimes wondered what happened to the Shirley Temple doll and thought, "They could have given her to me."

A short time later, I began to have a recurring bad dream. It was all mixed up with the new cartoon character, "Mickey Mouse" and his popular picture show <u>Steamboat Willie</u>. Of course as soon as it came to the Rialto, Daddy said we had to check it out. Most of the people there laughed a lot and were having a good time. I didn't laugh much and one scene really frightened me. There was a chase across a lot of mechanical equipment on the steamboat. Actually, I can't remember if Mickey was the chaser or being chased, but I put my hands over my eyes so I wouldn't see it. That didn't work; I still managed to peek through to see more than I wanted.

In my nightmare, I was running and jumping from machine to machine and the Mouse was chasing me. I knew if he caught me, it would be all over. Sometimes, Mrs. Prust joined Mickey in the chase. I always ran as fast as I could until it seemed I couldn't breath. They would surely catch me any minute. With every nightmare, I woke up just in the knick of time shaking all over, but safe in my own bed. Gradually, the dream disappeared from my sleep; only to reappear at unexpected times. Even now that mouse can slip back into my bed.

I realize now that death can be a difficult experience at any age, but, over the years I believe faith has helped me to reach a little better understanding of this troubling part of living.

One summer morning, close to my fifth birthday, Daddy said, "O.K., get ready, we're goin' to town this morning."

My mind started with questions. "Wonder what this is all about? We don't go to town on Saturday morning, we always go Saturday afternoon." Daddy usually drifted down to Parks Drug Store where the guys gathered to talk about "important stuff." Sometimes I'd stay with him and that was good for an ice cream cone. More often I went to the grocery store or the dry goods store with Mama. That was good for nothin' cause "you'd better not ruin your supper."

Our next stop would be the Rialto Theater where for the price of a dime I could cheer for Tom Mix or Gene or Hoppy to catch the rustlers, bank robbers and other bad guys.

I remember only one other time we went to town on Saturday morning. We went to the train depot. Some railroad cars were parked on a siding and inside a dead whale stretched down the length of three cars, which didn't impress Mama or me a whole lot, but Daddy was pretty excited..

What did impress me was the flea circus. To this day, I wonder how they trained those tiny hateful insects to push merry-go-rounds, swing in swings and do other tricks.

So, why were we headed for town on this Saturday morning? We passed both the drug store and the grocery story. The Rialto Theater wasn't even open for business. It was morning! As we pulled up at the end of Main Street in front of the depot, I thought, "Oh no! Not another whale! 'Course it could be another flea circus."

"Come on," laughed Daddy. He knew I was about to "bust" inside but wouldn't give even a little hint.

We walked though the depot to the platform out back. The sound of a whistle let us know a train was coming in. I watched it grind to a stop. No whale! No flea circus! "What's going on? Is someone on that train? Is Grandma coming to see us?"

"Wait here," said Daddy as he walked over to a boxcar and began talking to a man holding a lot of papers in his hand. He gave one of the papers to Daddy, slid open the boxcar door and jumped inside. He backed out dragging a big crate. He and Daddy took the crate off the car, and Daddy called me over.

"Hey, Toots, come over here and meet your new dog." I couldn't believe it. There inside the crate was a big red bear. No—not a bear; it was a dog! "She looks like a bear." "No," laughed Daddy, "she's a Chow dog, her name is Fanny and she's yours. Happy Birthday."

Fanny sat in the back seat beside me on the way home. I couldn't get enough of looking at her—so soft and pretty. She was looking at me, too. At last, I dared to reach out and touch her fur. She licked my fingers and I knew that this was a very special day for me, one I would never forget. A seed of love was planted in my heart and will flourish there forever.

Fanny became my best friend and we were always together that summer. Most often she lay under the Cottonwood tree watching the kids play. Sometimes she would join our games and run around barking at everyone. There were other dogs around, but Queen Fanny ruled the kingdom.

Sometimes Fanny and I would sit together, and I would wonder how a sky could be so blue, or how Fanny's fur could be so soft, or who made the cloud pictures floating across the sky? Sometimes we would wander the lease together. At least one time, we went too far. We walked through the woods farther and farther and before I knew it, we were down below the hill. I recognized the Gulf Camp and knew for sure it was way beyond my wanderings limit. Besides, I wasn't sure which way to go to get home again. I whispered to Fanny that we might be a little lost.

Finally, some guy who was cutting weeds asked me where I lived. Fanny lay down in front of me and growled deep in her throat. The guy didn't come any closer, but he did ask me if I might be lost, and asked me again where I lived.

I pointed in the direction of the woods and said, "Up somewhere on the hill, I think."

He laughed and said, "Aren't you the little Murphy girl? I know your Dad. Just follow that little path leading up through the trees. You'll be home in no time."

He turned back to the weeds. "Come on, Fanny, we better get home 'fore Mama misses us." We started up the path. True enough, before long we came out on the old red dirt road that led to my house. We reached the Cottonwood tree with Mama no where in sight. Fanny and I sat down to rest and as I petted her, I whispered in her ear, "Looks like we made it! This is a good thing!"

The next Spring about the time the Cottonwood fluff started "snowing", Daddy gave me something new to think about, "It looks like we're gonna get some puppies soon."

"Well", I thought, "this will mean another trip to the depot." Fanny came on the train, so I just figured the puppies would come on the train, too.

But it didn't happen that way at all. One morning when I got up, neither Daddy nor Fanny were in the house. "Where are they?" Mama said they were in the shed. I finished breakfast as fast as I could and jumped down to go outside. Without giving any reason why, Mama said I had to stay in the house. I ran to the window but couldn't see a thing. I waited and waited. After a really long time, Daddy came in with eyes shining and said, "Come on outside with me."

He took me straight to the shed and opened the door. I looked inside. "Oh my! Oh my, gosh!" Six little bears with their eyes shut tight were kinda pushing each other around and climbing all over each other. Fanny was there, too, very quiet, just watching. "How did they get here? Where did they come from? Did you go to the depot?" Daddy explained that they were Fanny's puppies. She had been carrying them around inside her tummy for awhile, and he had helped her get them to us. I guess that was my first lesson on the "birds and the bees" but right then, it was enough for me.

Every day I would visit them in the shed. I watched them shove each other around to get the milk Fanny had for them; I watched their eyes open. What a sight they were, it seemed as if every night they grew a little bigger. Soon they were barking like real puppies and running around outside the shed. Sometimes we rolled around together in the red dirt.

Other times in the early morning, Daddy would put the "bears" in my crib. We would have a great time together, always with Fanny standing nearby watching over things. (Mama wasn't real happy with this arrangement and before long, she said they were too big to put in the bed.)

When I started naming the puppies, Daddy explained that they couldn't stay at our house. We had to share them with other boys and girls, so one by one Daddy sold them. There were tears as each one left. I missed them; but told myself that they had looked happy with their new friends; besides, Fanny stayed with me, and as Daddy said, "Now, Toots, don't you worry none. Those puppies are gonna be OK."

That summer I turned six years old, and besides the puppies, there was something else to be excited about. It was almost time to start to school. What an adventure! There were no schools on our lease, so everyone rode the bus to the big brick school in Seminole. There were lots of swings and teeter-totters and merry-go-rounds in the yard. Several of these schools were built by the WPA in the 30's and many are still in use today.

I guess Mama went to the school and registered me for first grade. From the first day, I waited under the Cottonwood tree with Joan (who was also in first grade) and Don and all the other kids who lived on the hill. When the bus came, I found that first step was so high that I could barely even get on the bus. Because we were the first to be picked up, we all got seats. I liked that part.

The five-mile trip to town took about an hour, because we stopped so many times. By the time the gang of kids waiting at the Sinclair plant were picked up, the seats were full and many of the kids had to stand all the way to town.

I remember one tall, thin girl who smiled at me each day as she stood next to my seat. I think she knew I was a little scared because everything was so strange. This smiling girl made me feel a little better. She told me that her name was Mabel.

When we reached the school on the first day, several ladies were waiting out front. They called the first graders into one big group, then began calling out names. We separated into smaller groups and marched to our rooms. The teachers cautioned us to "pay attention, because tomorrow no one will meet you. You will have to find your rooms on your own."

With my group, I followed the teacher into a room, put my new lunch pail into a closet, sat down at my very own desk, and my education began.

As I looked around, I could see I was the only girl in the class wearing ugly long brown stockings. To keep them up, Mama pinned them to my pants. That was a real pain. (Remember, Mama was from central Illinois and when school started, it was a signal—time for long stockings.)

In Oklahoma when school started, they were surely not needed and certainly not wanted. I confess it didn't take long for those ugly stockings to find a place in my lunch pail and remain there till it was time to leave for home. I've wondered if Mama ever knew how seldom I wore those stockings all day long. Finally along about fourth grade, she decided Oklahoma lease kids didn't need to wear long, brown stockings.

One of my favorite school things was writing on the blackboard. Even though some of us could barely reach it, that's where we usually did our beginning adding and subtracting problems. Sometimes I finished before some of the others; I found that to be a good time to socialize. I would talk to anyone who would listen. The teacher (I don't remember her name) with exaggerated patience would plead, "Little Miss Murphy, would you please stop talking?" For a minute I would stand quietly, but before I could stop myself, I would be chattering again.

One day, Miss What's-her-name had had enough. She marched over, took my arm, gave me a couple of swats and said, "Now you sit down in your seat and be quiet! I don't want to hear another word, or you'll never go to the board again."

My feelings hurt much more than my bottom, and I had to wipe the tears on my sleeve. No Kleenex in those days and I always lost my hanky. I wish I could say I learned my lesson, but "talking out of turn" was a problem throughout my school years—sometimes even now.

Nor was this the only time I managed to embarrass myself quite royally. One fifth grade experience brings a painful memory. Music test time for fifth graders was always a comic disaster—especially when the boys sang their solos in quivering, changing voices. This particular music test happened on a rainy Oklahoma day and giggles from the girls were not setting real well with Miss Casselman. As each person stepped to the front of the room and tried to get through a verse of the test song, the "tee-hee-hees" sounded all over the room. Finally, Miss Casselman made a new rule, "The next person who makes a sound during the testing will be punished." Wouldn't you know! Harry Dobbs was the next person to sing. Now Harry was a nice boy, a little older than the rest of us, and well along into the voice-changing throes of puberty. He went to the front, cleared his throat a couple of times, and began. Almost immediately, his voice cracked through two or three octaves, and just as immediately a giggle bubbled right out of my lips.

I covered my mouth and tried to look innocent, but it didn't work. "Alright, Mildred, I warned all of you. Go to the cloak room and stay there until we are finished." I hadn't had my turn at singing yet, so this meant I would have no grade for the test.

In the cloakroom, which smelled like damp peanut butter sandwiches, I buried my face in my coat so the others wouldn't hear me cry. "Why, oh why, do I always do this? Why couldn't I keep from giggling—except he did sound really funny."

I didn't get to come out of that hateful room till the bell rang for lunch, and I still hate peanut butter sandwiches.

These little episodes didn't dampen my enthusiasm for school one bit. I had such a yearning for learning, especially for reading. I knew all the letters, but I wanted them to fit together into stories.

Every Sunday morning before church, Daddy would spread the funny papers out on the kitchen table. While I looked at the pictures, he read to me the words printed in the little balloons. It was our special time together. Even my nickname "Toots" came from the Ally Oop comic strip. Ally Oop's wife, Watootsie, wore her hair all drawn up into a bone. Mama would gather my poor straight hair into a pony tail on top of my head with a ribbon; so for Daddy, my name became "Toots." Nobody else ever called me that.

I wanted to surprise Daddy some Sunday morning and read the comic strips to him. Seems a lofty ambition for someone who was just on the beginning pages of McGuffey's Reader. But I knew I wouldn't give up because I was sure the words could unlock the doors to all kinds of wonderful mysteries.

Even as I grew up, Daddy never gave up the name "Toots," and because of that, I have one very treasured memory of my wedding. Daddy and I were waiting in the foyer of the small country church where James and I were married. A cold rain was falling that February day, and I kept fussing with my damp veil. It didn't seem quite right.

The piano sounded the entry notes to let us know everyone else was in place. It was time to begin the walk down the aisle. Daddy hesitated, then reached out and touched my cheek. (It seemed so unlike him.) "Let's go, Toots. It's gonna be OK." Little did I know that would be the last time I would hear those words from him on this earth. Less than three months after the wedding, with the suddenness of an Oklahoma tornado, he would be struck down— gone from my life.

Many years later on one of the most difficult days of my life, I heard the words echo one more time. My husband, James had a massive stroke early one morning. After spending hours at the hospital, the doctor finally sent me home very late that night. I was sitting on the floor with my arms around both my dogs. As I buried my face in their soft fur, a feeling of warm comfort filled my heart, and I heard the words, "Toots, It's gonna be OK." Imagination? The wind? God's angel? I only know it WAS my daddy's voice.

Now back to the "lease child."

Summer came and my pal Fanny and I began our wanderings on the lease again. The Oklahoma sun beat down and the red dust covered everything that summer and stayed until fall. It was hot! Week after week, the rain forgot us. On just such a day, Daddy came in from work with a surprise. "Let's get packed. It's time for a vacation. We're leaving for Illinois in the morning." Mama thought it was a good idea, she was homesick and besides, "it might be cooler up there." (It wasn't.)

Mama pulled out the old suitcase and began to sort out what we needed—everyday things, Sunday things, and some in-between things for me. I brushed Fanny and tried to tell her to get ready for a really long trip. (I still remembered that long, long bus ride.) Daddy tinkered with wires and parts under the hood of the car, which wasn't new but was a step up from the Model A he had driven across the Ozarks back in '33.

Sunrise found us on the road; sunset found us pulling into a row of one-room cabins. The big sign over the gate read, "Camp Joy." Mama had packed supper before we left and she spread it out on one of the tables under some trees. Mama and I agreed with Daddy, "Thelm', this tastes mighty good."

Twilight gives way quickly to night in the Ozarks and soon we were ready for bed. We would be leaving early again the next morning. One other thing I remember about this trip was Mama remarking several times, "We should have traveled at night, it would have been cooler."

At last we reached central Illinois. The relatives were glad to see us and it didn't take long for both sides of the family to plan the reunion picnics. Forty to fifty aunts, uncles and cousins plus one grandma at each gathering would spend a Sunday after church eating, playing games, singing, and eating again. One thing for sure, those families could really eat!

After a big kiss or a pinch on the cheek, "My, how you've grown," became a worn-out greeting, but I guess a person does grow some when it's been two years between visits. Most of the relatives lived on farms and that was my favorite place to visit.

Grandma Corie lived in Clarksville, a little place with only two stores (one had been owned by my grandfather who also drove a huckster wagon). The blacksmith shop on the corner was still in business and students still attended the grade school which both my mom and dad attended and where my other grandmother had been a teacher.

The little house where I had been born stood at the end of the lane that ran beside my grandfather's store. I wish I would have walked down there, and now it's too late. It's been torn down, along with my Grandpa's store and the blacksmith shop. Only Grandma Corie's house is left.

The two weeks flew by. The last family reunion was over, the last fried chicken drumstick and the last piece of corn-on-the-cob had been eaten. It had been a couple of fun weeks, but the goodbyes had been said. We were leaving for home the next morning.

That last afternoon I was sitting in front of Grandma's house. It was cool there under the big oak trees and I was thinking about going home. I was anxious to go because I knew school had already started.

Fanny was lying at the side of the road by the row of mailboxes not far from me. I thought, "I just bet she's ready to go home, too. I'll go over and ask her." As I stood up, I heard a loud rumbling sound and looked up to see a cloud of white dust swirling up from the graveled road. A scream cut through the quiet of the afternoon. The scream was mine. Like a scary movie in slow motion, I watched the truck pull across the road straight toward Fanny. She raised her head but had no time to move. Both of those big front and back wheels rolled over her. The driver looked right at me, then he pulled the steering wheel the other way and the truck roared out of sight leaving the white dust still swirling over everything.

"NO! NO! NO!" I ran to Fanny. I wanted to reach out to her, but I couldn't do it. She lay there all smashed and bloody—not moving. Daddy came running across the road from the store shouting. He had seen the whole ugly thing. He put his arms around me trying to quiet my wild sobbing, but I was not to be consoled. "How could that bad man do this? Fanny wasn't even in the road. I know she's dead. Dead! Daddy, how could he kill my dog?"

Daddy had no answers for my questions. He said very quietly, "She never liked too much sun. We'll bury her in a nice shady place." And we did. The vacation was over.

Since that time, I've learned that there is often a risk in loving. But I believe, that no matter how much it hurts, it is better to take that risk with love in my life than to live in the emptiness of a life without love.

We left for home the next morning. For some reason the back seat of our car was packed so full that there was only a little space between all the stuff and the ceiling. I didn't ask about it; I didn't care. I sat in the front seat between Mama and Daddy part of the time. Most of the way I crawled into that little cave in the back seat, buried my head in the blanket and quietly cried for my lost friend—my big "bear" dog. Mama and Daddy were very quiet; I thought they were like me—missing Fanny. I didn't know about the surprise waiting for me at the top of our hill.

When we drove through Seminole a couple of days later, night had come. We reached the lease and drove slowly up the rutted hill. It was dark at the top and I strained my eyes trying to see my house. How could this be? It seemed like it wasn't there. In fact, Gilkey's house and the bunkhouse seemed to be missing, too. "Where's our house?" No one answered. "I think somebody took our house."

Daddy stopped on the sandy spot where we played. The car lights shone on a charred post standing as a black sentinel guarding a big pile of ashes. "Tell me what happened!" I screamed, "who did this? Where is our house? Where is my stuff?"

By this time, Mama was crying too. "The house burned down while we were gone. So did Gilkey's house and the bunkhouse."

Sure enough! Nothing but ashes and twisted metal remained. With no way to stop the flames, fire had destroyed three of the houses on the hill. Nothing had been saved. Mama cried for her new Montgomery Ward stove and icebox (bought on payments; no insurance).

Daddy patted Mama and said, "Tomorrow we'll come and see if anything is left under the ashes. Maybe we can find a few things. Bob and Lizzie said we could stay with them tonight."

Then he came over where I was standing in the ashes. He stooped down and surrounded me with his strong arms. As I buried my face in his shoulder, I sobbed, "Daddy, what's fair about this? First that mean ole truck kills my dog, now my bed is all twisted and burned. Why? Why is this happening?" With a voice that never wavered, he promised, "You'll see, Toots. It's gonna be OK."

PART TWO

Down Under The Hill

It was time to leave the ashes on the hill. As we climbed into the car, Mama urged, "Get up here with us," but I said, "No." I just wanted to slip into my "cave" in the back seat and hide my face again.

As Daddy backed the car around, and we started down the hill, I tried not to cry. "Where could we go?" I wondered. Daddy had promised, "It's gonna be OK," but how could it be OK? Everything was gone—my bed, my school clothes, all our things.

Aunt Lizzie always said, "Say a prayer when things look bad." But when had it ever looked this bad? Besides the only prayers I knew were "thank you for this food" and "now I lay me down to sleep." Neither of these fit what was happening as we bumped down the hill away from the place that had become home for me.

The Davises lived on the first road north of the Sinclair lease so we were soon pulling into their driveway. Bob worked with Daddy at Plant 12; they had become our first friends after we became "Okies." I guess they'd been expecting us because everyone was waiting in the front yard—Bob and Lizzie, their daughter Betty Ann, and Lizzie's sisters, Joy and Janelle.

After a lot of hugging and crying, we went inside. Lizzie pointed to the quilt pallets laid out on the closed-in front porch. "I thought the kids could sleep here on the porch. The nights are still warm; they'll be fine out here, don't you think?" Mama just nodded her head. (Janelle was not really a kid, she was already training to be a hairdresser in Seminole. She liked to practice her styles on us; but though she tried, she couldn't do much with my Dutch bob.)

For a long time after we crawled into our pallets that awful night, I could hear the grown-ups talking over coffee in the kitchen. Sometimes I could hear Daddy laugh, and gradually I drifted off to sleep to that reassuring sound.

Mama had enrolled me in school before vacation and it had already started, so right after breakfast the next morning, Betty Ann, Joy and I walked down to the corner to catch the school bus. It turned out to be the same bus I rode before, with the most of the same kids. All except Joan; her Daddy had found a house for them in town. I was glad to see that Mabel still rode my bus. She smiled in her shy way as she said, "I'm sorry your house burned down."

Lucky for me, Oklahoma fall days were usually warm and sunny, and my summer "vacation" clothes were O.K. to wear to school for awhile. (At least those ugly, long brown stockings were gone. I could only hope the Oklahoma stores didn't sell such awful socks.) Mama explained, "Most of your Daddy's work clothes were lost in the fire, so any new things for you or me will just have to wait."

One day I jumped off the school bus and found a big surprise waiting. Mama held out a package saying, "This came today and it has your name on it. It's from your Aunt Stella." (Aunt Stella was Mama's sister who was a nurse in Chicago. I couldn't even imagine where Chicago might be, but I did remember Aunt Stella.)

Everyone gathered round. Betty Ann was jumping up and down shouting, "Open it! Let me help. Open it!"

I struggled with the twine wrapped around the package. Someone brought scissors and finally the package came open. Five pieces of brightly colored material fell out. "What in the world?" Then I saw the patterns and Mama said, "Well, just look at this. We can make you some new dresses." She read the note inside. "Stella says this green piece is to make you a coat and just like I thought, the other pieces are for dresses." She seemed to be as excited as I was.

Betty Ann's smile kind of faded as she said, "I've never ever gotten four new dresses at the same time." I might have shared one with her, but she was a little older and a lot bigger than I was and there wasn't enough material to make her a dress. (To tell the truth, I probably wouldn't have shared anyway.)

They were so pretty—all bright different colors, but one piece was really special. White sailors were scattered over a bright red background. There was some blue tape to add decoration. I asked Mama if she would make my "sailor" dress first. She did just that, and when she finished she found a piece of blue silky material and made a sailor tie to wear with it. I thought it was the grandest dress I'd ever seen.

Who could ever believe this—four new dresses at one time; and a coat, too. Aunt Stella was a magic fairy godmother who could grant wishes beyond my imagination. With Daddy's help, I printed a thank you letter and we put a stamp on it and sent it all the way to Chicago.

Mama used Lizzie's sewing machine to make the dresses, and every day I ran from the bus stop as fast as I could to see if any were done yet. Mama said we would save them for "Sunday" dresses, but sometimes she might let me wear one to school. (I thought that sounded pretty good seein' as how the only other dresses I had were a few hand-me-downs.) Of course, I had to promise to keep the new dresses clean and heaven forbid if I should tear one. I tried my hardest!

I also tried not to be too proud. I remembered what Aunt Lizzie had said about pride and falling. I sure didn't want to fall down and tear one of those new dresses.

Mama made all the dresses a little big so they would last a long time. The sailor dress was always my favorite; in fact, in a fourth grade class picture there I am on the front row still wearing it. Of course, by fourth grade it was kinda' short and the sailors were fading away.

Around Halloween, some rig worker was transferred to another oil field, and we moved into the house he left behind. It was another unpainted shotgun house "with a path" out back, but it was surely better than the tents and even chicken houses that had been homes to some of the workers in the early oil boom days. Also, it was getting crowded at the Davises.

Our "new" home had the usual three rooms, but one thing was different. A floor-to-ceiling partition separated the eating/cooking area from the sink/ice box area. I never figured out why, but convenience was never a requirement for boomshacks. Most people were just glad to have a house to live in.

Mama and Daddy's bedroom was next to the kitchen. I slept in the front room on a couch which opened out (when it worked) to make a bed. No one but me seemed to mind the big crack down the middle. It would be several years before I would have a "real" bed again.

A bonus to the house was a big front porch with a roof and a railing. On a hot day, the porch was nice because there were no shady Cottonwoods or any other kinds of trees around. The steps were a good place to sit and think and watch the fluffy white cloud pictures race across the blue, blue sky. The yard was a patch of sticker burrs and goatheads. It took up a lot of my time just pulling them out of my feet. (Except for school and Sunday school, wearing shoes was <u>never</u> a part of my attire.)

Another bonus were the two steel cables that crossed over the roof of the house. They were cemented into the ground and literally held the house down. We found out what a good idea this was the next spring. One Sunday afternoon, while we were visiting some friends in Sasakwa, a tornado cut a narrow path across the lease. It didn't seem to do a lot of damage, but it did tear away the roof of our house on each end back to the cables. The center part of the roof and the rest of the house seemed to be OK.

When Mama saw what had happened, she "made a real fit." "Now, Lucian, will you just tell me what you're going to do about this mess!" Daddy gave her a peck on the cheek and came up with his usual answer, "Now, 'Spanky', just calm down. It's gonna be OK. We can fix it easy." Spanky was Daddy's nickname for Mama from "Our Gang Comedy," and usually when he called her that, she just got madder.

This time she stomped away muttering, "I'm tired of this OK stuff." Daddy went to get Mr. Stewart and a couple of other guys to help him. Before dark caught them, they had temporary coverings on the roof until it could be patched later.

The tornado hadn't dumped too much rain, so the damage inside the house wasn't great. My bed was a little damp, but better that than to be blown away. In all our years of living in "tornado alley," that's the closest we ever came to being caught in one. That's not to say we didn't sometimes see them swirling in the distance.

This lease had more houses than the other one. A couple of other shotgun houses were near ours; and on a hill just above us were three rows of company houses with the plant sitting at the top. A red dirt road zigzagged back and forth in front of these nicer company houses. During the rainy season, Sinclair dump trucks would haul in loads of rock to keep the muddy quagmires passable. This did not keep rivers of water from draining down the hills and making little red ponds at the bottom (usually in our back yard).

There were no drilling rigs on this site, but several nearby wells kept the nighttime lullabies going since they never stopped pumping to send the oil up to the gasoline plant. Even today a sniff of fresh crude oil can instantly trigger the picture of that suntanned, barefoot little girl running, always running up and down the red dirt roads. Sometimes the memory is so real I almost need to sit down and rest.

We lived in a community of Sinclair workers. The people had come from many different towns and states, even countries; leaving family and friends behind. They had found new friends on the lease and became family for each other—the Stewarts, the Lavins, the Seifrieds, the Hooseapples, the Hendricksons, and now, the Murphys. These new friends welcomed our family into the group with furniture and bedding and pots and pans and other things needed to replace the necessities that had been lost in the fire.

I found a Lil' Orphan Annie mug in one of the boxes of dishes and this became a treasure. Sometimes as a special treat, Mama would fill it with Ovaltine and I would join her and Daddy for "coffee." Of course, this meant Mama and I had to listen to Daddy give his best imitation of Annie's dog, Sandy. "Arf! Arf!" It was supposed to be funny, so Mama laughed politely and I laughed because I thought it **was** funny.

I guess many people would have considered us poor; but we had a place to live, were never hungry for lack of food, and Daddy had a job. I never once thought about being "poor." I know that at suppertime Daddy always thanked the Lord for all of our blessings.

Each morning Doris Faye Stewart, Norma Jean Lockhart and I walked up to the top of the hill to the bus stop. The first morning, there it was, still that same bus I'd been riding before. The only surprise was to discover that Mabel, my "big girl" friend lived in one of the company houses in the first row just above ours.

I soon found out that one of the best parts of living "down under the hill" was the number of kids around. They were all ages and sizes, and everyone played together in the evenings after school. Anyone new was welcomed.

Punch-The-Icebox, Sheep-of-My-Pen, and Piggy-Wants-A-Motion were all versions of the old favorite game, Hide-n'-Seek. One thing for sure, seven years old was the bottom of the age range and I got caught early in the game. If I was "it", I was usually "it" forever 'cause even when I caught someone for the pen, escape was no problem with the help of a friend's motion. No challenge there!

Play went on till bedtime when someone's Mama called out, "Come on in now. It's already bedtime." One of the kids would shout, "All's out's in free." That meant the game really was over. Too bad if you hid out of hearing range. You might "slip in" to base only to discover that everyone had already gone home.

There can be no doubt about the influence of the Rialto's weekly western movie on the games that we played. Cowboys and Indians rated high on the list and the weapon of choice was the homemade rubber gun. With a piece of wood, a clothes pin and an old innertube to make ammunition, everyone could join in the fun. These guns could get pretty fancy and some of the boys made double-barrel and long barrel rifle guns. The older boys always had a new gun in progress. They worked for hours sawing and carving the wood till the gun was "just right." Sometimes they would give their old guns to the younger kids who might not have one.

I had my own gun. Daddy had made it special with "Toots" carved on the handle. I never really got close enough to shoot anyone. There was a very good reason for this. If I was close enough to shoot another cowboy or Indian, that meant the kid could shoot back. Those rubber strips could HURT! Even more so if the shooter had tied a couple of knots in the strip of rubber.

Usually I just galloped around, whipping up my pretend horse to breathtaking speeds and yelling at the top of my voice. It was always fun to reveal someone's hiding place by yelling out, "Hey, Joe, you better watch out! Here comes that Lavin kid and he's got help with him." Then I would gallop away leaving Joe sputtering. Of course, this meant that I had to be very careful not to get in Joe's shooting range the rest of the game.

I liked to be on the Indians' side because Bob-o Hendrickson was always the Indian chief. His mom was a Seminole Indian so, of course, he was right for the part. He was about twelve years old and to my worshipful eyes, he was at least as good as Tom Mix, surely better than Bob Steele. In our games, the Indians won as often as the Cowboys.

The rubber guns game plan was to duck behind bushes, wash houses, trees or whatever was handy until you had a chance to "shoot" the enemy. When you were shot, you were captured and taken hostage into camp. You could be rescued, otherwise you were out of the game.

My personal plan was to gallop around and stay out of range. If the battle got too fierce, my backup plan was to go into someone's house for a drink of water. As I think back, it surely must say something about the place or the times, when the older boys and girls would tolerate the younger ones like me, and play their games around us.

I still liked to wander around the lease by myself. Seems like there was always a lot to see. Mama would warn me, "Don't go into the thicket. The goat man will get you!" Maybe it was because I was a little older, or a little less brave, or because I had heard all the stories the other kids told about the old goat man who lived in the thicket; but, I do know that this time Mama's warning carried some weight with me and I stayed away.

Until one fateful day when the idea just popped into my head, "I don't have anything to do today." I thought a little more and decided, "I bet this would be a good time for me to see if that old goat man really does live in that thicket. Maybe I can see some baby goats from the edge of the trees."

A deep gully cut across the path to the thicket. It became a red raging torrent during the spring and fall rains, but the rest of the year the bottom was dry red dust. There was no bridge, just some pipelines that crossed from one side to the other. I wasn't too brave about "high-wire" circus action, so I always sat down on the biggest pipeline and scooted across the yawning emptiness. I never looked down until I was safe on the other side. (I would deal with Mama's questions about my rusty pants later.)

As I walked toward the woods, I thought about all the stories the older kids told on summer evenings—"he" never comes out of the thicket, "he" lives in a shack with the goats, no one knows his name, and other, scarier stuff.

I wondered about the goat man. "Did he really like to live back there? Did he really have goats? If he never came out, what did he eat? Did he ever have a little girl like me? Why was he back there anyway? Was he even real?"

When I came to the edge of the woods, I stopped. I tried to see through the trees. "Should I go on?" I took a few more steps along the path. I stopped again. "What was that sound? Was that a bell tinkling? It sounded like a bell. Maybe I should run."

I took a few more steps, pulled back a branch and took one more look. "Maybe a baby goat was lost in the thicket? Should I go find it?"

Then before I could decide what to do, I saw HIM! He was leaning against a tree, just looking at me, not moving. His long gray hair and beard looked tangled. It had to be the old goat man because a baby goat was nuzzling against his hand.

A finger of fear touched me; I didn't wait for answers to my questions. Aunt Lizzie's prayer idea kicked in, "Get me out of here, NOW!" I turned and ran as fast as I could. Even though I had a terrible pain in my side, I never stopped till I reached the pipelines crossing the gully. I sat down for a minute and sneaked a peek back toward the thicket. Nothing but the edge of the wood showed in the distance. There was no sound of tinkling bells or anything else. With no more hesitation, I scooted back across the gully and headed home.

I never talked about this to anyone. I don't remember how I explained the rusty pants to Mama. Maybe she didn't ask.

I never went back into the thicket; but I never stopped wondering about that day. Did I really see someone or something? Or did my overactive imagination create that specter in the woods. One thing I would like to know; if he really did live there, what terrible sadness caused this man to choose the company of his goats deep in the thicket over that of his "fellow" men in the world.

As spring evenings grew longer, Daddy would say, "I'm going to give the bass at Danielson's Lake a try. Wanna come along?" Well, sure I did. I would run to find my mayonnaise jar, and I would be ready.

We'd go by Davises to pick up Bob and Betty Ann and head for the lake. Betty Ann and I would compare the lids on the jars and decided which one had the most holes. These were our lightening bug lanterns.

Other kids were usually on the beach with their jars and as soon as the sun dipped to the edge of the water, our fun began. Hundreds of lightening bugs turned on their lanterns in the gathering darkness. As the Daddies made their way around the lake trying to fool the bass with their lures, we would run in all directions lured by the luminescent green and gold bugs.

The goal was to see who could capture the most glowing bugs to put in the jar. As darkness deepened, the risks increased. Away from the beach, the brambles snatched at bare skin, logs flew up and barked the shins, and sometimes the lake moved right into the path. What a disaster if the lid was open on the jar when the bug hunter fell into the water.

As the bass went back to their hidden hollows, the fishermen drifted to the beach fire to drink their coffee and exchange stories of "the granddaddy that got away."

We kids stayed just outside the circle of the fire, with our jars lined up in a row. We compared the glow in the jars. "Who had captured the most lightening bugs?" How deceiving they were. When I opened my lid to let them fly free, there was no warmth, no shared light for my path, only a moment's beauty to be remembered. The next time Daddy went to plug for bass, I knew I would be there, too, chasing lightening bugs.

Life can offer a few firefly experiences. Sometimes I still chase the glow, only to discover that when I catch up to it, the light and warmth that seemed so beautiful is only a promise—left unfulfilled.

Not long after we settled into the new house, Daddy brought home a new surprise, a beautiful male Chow dog, named Chang. He was not a puppy, and was bigger than Fanny had been. It took awhile for us to become friends. For a long time when he lay down beside me, he would be just beyond my reach. We finally came to an understanding; he would let me scratch behind his ears while I talked to him, but I was not to hug him tight or try to hold him down. That would bring a little growl from him, certainly not a friendly sound, but I wasn't afraid. I knew the rules.

Then the "bad" thing happened. One hot afternoon, Chang was with me in the back yard when Beau, our paper boy, came to collect. Mama came to the door, then went back into the house to get the money. Beau and I were talking when he decided to shake his paper bag at Chang in a threatening way. There was a deep growl, but Chang didn't move.

"You better not do that, Beau. Chang doesn't like it."

Beau just laughed and said, "Aw, he won't do anything. Watch this." He swung the paper bag which just grazed Chang across the back. The dog reacted immediately and went toward Beau. Just then Mama came out of the house screaming at the dog. "Stop it! Chang, stop it!"

I was screaming too, "Don't hurt my dog. You hear me? Don't you dare hurt my dog."

When it was all over, Chang had bitten Beau's hand (a small cut); then he had run over and knocked Mama down. Beau saw his chance and ran out the gate toward home. I ran over to Mama; Chang ran to the corner of the yard where he lay down.

Mama was O.K.—just blazing mad at that "damn" dog.

"Oh boy, Mama is REALLY mad. Chang, we'd better stay out of her way 'till Daddy gets home."

It didn't look like things were gonna get much better. When Daddy came in, his face looked like a storm cloud. He said Beau's hand was O.K. and Beau's dad (Mama's cousin) had said, "Beau should have known better than to tease the dog."

After Daddy made sure that Mama was O.K., he came out on the steps and sat down beside me. I had a bad feeling in my stomach. I knew I wasn't going to like what he had to say. It was almost never a good thing when he was so serious.

"Toots, you know that Chang did a bad thing." I just shook my head. I really didn't want to talk about this. "You know that we can't keep him. He might hurt you, or someone else."

"But, Daddy, Chang didn't hurt me today. He never would. And I know that he didn't mean to knock Mama down. Besides, I told Beau not to hit him."

"We just can't take the chance. We'll find a good home for him. It's gonna be OK."

Daddy took Chang away the next day. I'm really not sure what happened to him. Daddy just said he found a place for him. I do know one thing. This time Daddy was wrong. It wasn't OK! Even though he hadn't been a really good friend like Fanny, I still missed Chang. Even worse than that, as long as I lived at home, I never did have another dog. Mama wouldn't hear of it. Sometimes I would see a puppy and ask if we could have it; but her answer was always the same, "No! Not now! Not ever! Do you hear me? Not ever!"

Reading was still my very favorite part of school, and with each book I read, my world grew. Aunt Stella was well-known for her love of reading. My grandparents had farmed the bottom land of the Wabash River on the Illinois side. With a family of eight children born in a ten-year span, Mama said, "The chores were never finished; especially since Stella would disappear into whatever tree was handy so that she could read her books. Sometimes it was suppertime or later before she would decide to come down."

It was pretty clear that Mama was not happy with Aunt Stella about all this. "Mom never did a thing about Stella skipping her chores. Somebody else would have to do them and it was usually me," remembered Mama. "I guess they never thought that I might like to read a book, too."

I don't think this memory was a good one for Mama because sometimes she would say to me in her I-mean-business voice, "I could use a little help around here. Put that fool book away."

Aunt Stella always talked to me about the wonders of reading and for several years every birthday and Christmas meant the arrival of a book from Chicago. I still have a tattered copy of Uncle Tom's Cabin inscribed "From Aunt Stella—1937". Pretty sophisticated reading for a third grader. The human rights message was totally lost; but I did feel a kinship with "Topsy" and the way she "just growed." My all time favorite book from her was Kipling's The Jungle Book and Mowgli's Friends, especially that rascal mongoose, Rikki Tikki Tavi. Sometimes I still like to revisit Mowgli and his friends of the jungle.

The most spectacular event of the "Down Under the Hill" years began for me in a small way. It changed my world forever.

I got the first hint one evening after supper. It seemed kinda' quiet around the house. I was out on the front steps coloring pictures in my new coloring book when Daddy came out and sat down beside me. "Wanna color with me, Daddy?"

"Naw," he said and sat there for awhile. Then he sort of blurted out, "We're gonna get a baby at our house."

"Yeah? When? When's this baby coming?"

"Not for awhile. Not till summer."

"O.K., but where's this baby coming from?" "Maybe on the train?" I wondered. "Lots of stuff comes on the train."

Daddy didn't give a really clear answer to my question. Instead he suggested, "Why don't you finish your picture now. We'll talk about this later."

As late fall slipped into winter and winter slipped into spring, nobody really talked much about the baby, but I sure hadn't forgotten. I noticed that Mama seemed to be getting fatter and she got a new dress to wear to church. I had too much going on to wonder for long why Mama was getting fatter. After all, Mamas did that sometimes.

One evening I noticed she was knitting a tiny sweater, I wondered, "Mama, that sweater sure isn't big enough for me. Whatcha' gonna do with it?"

"Oh, well, it's for the new baby." I waited for her to say more, but she didn't. She just went ahead with her knitting.

School closed for the summer—still no baby. I asked Mama, "Where is that baby that's supposed to be coming." Her reply was, "It's such a nice day, Mildred. Why don't you go outside and play."

When I asked Daddy about the baby, he just said, "One of these days soon."

I'm tellin' ya, I was about to give up; maybe that baby went to live with some other family. Lavins had a new baby. Maybe our baby went to live at their house.

Then one really hot morning, Daddy came to the door and called out to me, "Hey, Toots, come here, will you?" He seemed in a hurry.

I ran to the door. "Whatcha' want?"

"Run up the hill and ask Mrs. Seifried to come down. Just tell her it's time." It was June 14, 1936, and that Oklahoma sun was setting heat records every day.

And now Daddy wanted me to RUN! "What do you want Mrs. Seifried for, Daddy? It's really hot. Can't I just go up to the fence and holler for her and then come back?"

"Toots, go NOW. Just tell her to come. You stay up there, just sit on their back steps and when we want you, we'll let you know. Just watch for

Mrs. Seifried. She'll wave a towel, or something to let you know when you can come home. There will be a surprise waiting. Now GO!"

The tone of his voice said I'd better get going, so I ran up the hill. "Mrs. Seifried, Daddy says you should come down to our house right now. It's time." She seemed really happy. "Good glory," she said, "it's about time."

She told me to watch for her signal, but added that it would be quite awhile. If I got hungry while I waited, I should ask Mabel for a sandwich and a glass of milk. She gave me a big hug, hurried down the path and disappeared through our back door.

I sat down to wait and wonder and wonder and wait. Was this a game? We'd never played a game like this before. Mable called out from the kitchen, "Would you like a sandwich, there's plenty of time." Was she ever right!

After I ate my sandwich, we played a game of checkers and I think she let me win. I kept wondering why I couldn't go home. Finally I went back out on the steps. The shade stretched further and further down my legs; it was getting later and later.

What could be happening down there at my house? Maybe I should go see. Maybe they had forgotten all about me and my surprise. Still I waited. Mabel came out of the house with a glass of water and a cookie. She had one for me, too.

I took little bites to make my cookie last longer. "Mabel, do you think I should go down there? Maybe they forgot me. Maybe they went somewhere without me. I think I should go home now."

Mabel just smiled. "No they didn't go anywhere without you. Try to wait just a little bit more. It shouldn't be much longer before you can go home."

We sat together without saying anything. She never did talk very much. "Maybe I'll just take a little nap," I thought as I leaned against her.

Before I knew it, she was shaking my arm. "Wake up! Look, there's Mama giving your signal. You'd better scoot home right now."

I could see Mrs. Seifried standing in our back yard waving that towel in all directions. It **was** my signal. I climbed through the fence and ran down the hill as fast as I could. Mrs. Seifreid caught me in her arms and said, "Come on in and see who's here."

What did she mean, "Who's here?" I ran in—nobody in the kitchen. Into the bedroom—and stopped short. There was Mama in bed; Daddy was standing nearby smiling all over his face. He pointed toward a basket, "Come on over, Toots. Say hello to your new baby sister!"

"Oh, my!" I stumbled as I ran over. I looked in. "Oh, my, oh my gosh!"

What a disappointment! She was really little and she was red and wrinkled. While I stood there looking with unbelieving eyes, she screwed up her face and started crying. Daddy picked her up and rocked her in his arms; he'd forgotten all about me.

I ran out to the front steps and just sat there with my eyes squeezed shut—I sure wasn't gonna cry. Babies cry! I listened. That new baby sure could cry.

After a while Daddy came out and sat beside me. He didn't say anything at first. He just sat there. Then he pulled me close to him and sort of whispered, "Toots, I guess maybe you're a little disappointed right now."

"But Daddy, that ole baby can't even play with me. I thought she would play with me."

"I know, but just wait. Before you can even say 'Abracadabra', she'll be ready to play with you. You'll see. Every day she'll grow a little."

I didn't say anything, just sniffed my nose a little. But I knew for sure I wasn't gonna cry!

"You know something? Your new little sister needs a name," Daddy went on. "What do you think we should call her?"

Was he really asking me? Why would he ask me that? She wasn't my baby. But when he didn't say anymore, I thought about it for awhile. "Well, maybe we could name her for my best friends—Norma June Weinsburg and Norma Jean Lockhart. I really like them. What do you think, Daddy, maybe we could name her June Norma." Well that didn't sound right.

"Naw, not June Norma, that doesn't sound right." I thought some more, "Hey, Daddy, maybe we could call her Norma June. How do you think that sounds?"

"Why don't we see what your Mama says?" We went into the bedroom. I'd kind of forgotten that Mama was in bed. There was a fan blowing across a pan of water. Now, I wondered if she was sick.

They explained that she wasn't sick, just tired and needed to rest for a few days. I was so excited about naming the baby that I didn't give that any more thought.

"Thelm', Toots here has a name for the baby—it's Norma June. What do you think?"

They didn't even talk about it. "Sounds OK. to me," said Mama. She gave me a little smile and closed her eyes.

Here I was only seven years old, and they let me name the baby! My sister has never agreed that my choice was a good one and she doesn't hesitate to let me know this. I just tell her, "Too bad, you were too busy squallin' to have any input."

Daddy was right about the "OK" part. Though it took a while and some serious effort from both of us, it did become OK. The growing up together wasn't always fun. There were fierce arguments and hateful words sometimes, but we seem to have found the way to friendship with each other in these later years. (Right, Norma June?)

That fall, after the baby came, it was vacation time again. This time the ride was a little different. The dog was gone, but I still wasn't in the back seat of the car by myself—there in her big basket was the baby—Norma June. She had grown quite a bit, and sometimes I thought she might even be looking at me with a little smile. Of course she had to have a ribbon in her hair so Mama had tied it around the blonde curl on the top of June's head. (Only three months old and already she had a curl.)

The real surprise came when we reached Grandma's house in Illinois. Mama and Daddy had not told a single person about the baby—not even Grandma. Everyone was fit to be tied. (My aunt told me recently that none of them could believe their eyes when Daddy walked in with that baby in a basket.)

I've always wondered why they didn't tell anyone, but I know one thing; if they were looking to create a sensational surprise, they were successful. Every place we went, the relatives gathered round the basket, and the "ohs and ahs" could be heard all over the house.

Because everyone was so interested in Baby June, after a quick hello kiss from the aunts and a pat on the head from the uncles, I was left pretty much to myself. No problem there. When we visited at Aunt Lizzie's house, I got to see my cousin Maurice, who was a year older than I. We always had great adventures together.

After breakfast, he would show up at Aunt Lizzie's house with his dog, Trixie, and we started our day. Sometimes we would jump in Cousin Roger's soapbox derby car and go all over town—racing downhill and pushing uphill. We'd stop by Aunt Lizzie's flower garden to make a few Hollyhock dolls to ride along with us. I called them "southern" ladies with their sweeping skirts.

As dinner time came closer, we made sure we were near Murphy's General grocery store. After parking the soapbox car on the sidewalk in front of the store, we would go inside. After Uncle Theron (Maurice's dad) told a few jokes, he would ask, "Do you need a little something to tide you over till suppertime? Maybe a sandwich or a hunk of cheese?"

On his way to the meat counter he'd stop by the pop cooler and pull out a couple of Grapettes (he knew what we liked best). "A person's gotta have something that can wet their whistle on a hot day," he would say.

At the meat counter he'd pick up his big meat knife and cut a couple of thick slices of baloney with an extra slice for Trixie. We'd left her outside to guard the soapbox car. He kept an open loaf of bread nearby and before we knew it, Maurice and I had a picnic lunch. We loaded up the soapbox derby car and headed for the nearest shade tree. By now, the Hollyhock ladies had wilted and were left behind.

We made sure we saved one afternoon to explore Aunt Lizzie's attic. So many memories from earlier times filled the spaces. (When I became a Mama with babies of my own, I remembered an old cradle that was in Aunt Lizzie's attic. It had been Daddy's cradle, and Aunt Lizzie's daughter gave it to me. It is still a family treasure.)

That was the summer Maurice and I found the old Edison Amberola music box. What fun! We would put one of the cylinders on the arm, crank it up and listen to the strange scratchy music coming through the horn. Sometimes we would try to sing the songs, but usually just ended up laughing. (I still have the music box and the cylinders, and know now that we'd been listening to original recordings of Enrico Caruso and other well-known musicians.

The best place to go for a little rest was down in Aunt Lizzie's basement. We hoped she'd be there, and usually she was. "I see you two have been out wandering around again. You must be about tuckered. How about a cookie and a little fresh buttermilk? Here." She would chuckle as she took the lid off the cookie jar, and dipped the buttermilk out of the crock. Then she would go back to her work.

While we munched on the cookies, we could watch from the cool shadows as the shuttle of her loom flew back and forth. Sometimes she would laugh, "You two are always going places in Roger's car. Tell me now, where would you like to go on this magic flying carpet I'm weaving?"

Maurice and I tried to think, "Where could this magic carpet take us?" We couldn't seem to agree on a definite choice. I think that we had such a hard time because somehow we knew, without really knowing it, that sitting in Aunt Lizzie's basement with buttermilk and cookies was about as good as it gets.

That was a great vacation—one of the best ever, but as always, one morning Daddy asked, "Well, Toots, are you ready for the long ride home?" It was time to head southwest again. Old Route 66 was a better road now. The Ozark Mountains hadn't moved and the hairpin curves still circled around them, but at least the gravel was gone, replaced with a hard road. This helped keep the dust out of my eyes when Mama and Daddy rolled down the windows to let the wind blow out the heat.

We were all glad to get home that year, even Mama. Things settled into a routine. I started to school again, Daddy went to work, and Mama took care of the baby. By winter "the baby" was taking on a personality; she was becoming June. She would laugh right out loud when we played peek-a-boo. I thought, "Maybe this baby won't be too bad after all." Little did I know what the future held.

It was great fun to push her around the house in her four-wheeled walker. We would get a running start at the front door, straight through the bedroom and into the kitchen. I finally figured out the reason for the partition in the kitchen. We would skid past Mama who was getting supper, slow down just a little as we made the turn around the partition, pick up speed past the sink, then head for the front door.

"Hey, Mama, watch this!" and off we would fly at breakneck speed till we reached the front door. "You watch it yourself, you're gonna turn that thing over and hurt the baby." But all was well until Grandma Corie came from Illinois to spend the winter months with us.

Daddy's mother had died when he was born, and Grandpa was left with three boys, the oldest just three years old. The boys were cared for by aunts for a few years, but when Daddy was about six years old, Grandpa married a "spinster" to care for his boys. That spinster was Grandma Corie, who really had never been around children. It's been said by the relatives that she was faced with an impossible task; but for Grandma Corie there were no impossible tasks. She was no bigger than a minute, but her determination made up for lack of size.

When she came to visit us, she was quite old and her patience was pretty well used up. At least that's the way it seemed to this eight-year-old. I just knew she made problems for me. First of all, there was no place for her to sleep except on my couch with me. Second of all, morning found her sleeping all the way over on my side. The only reason I didn't fall off the couch was that it was against the wall. Third of all, she snored really loud.

It did no good to discuss these things with Daddy because he always said, "Toots, she's here and she's your grandma. You know, you are making your own trouble. Just settle down, and before you know it, she will be gone." And then he would add as usual, "It's gonna be OK." This time, I didn't want to hear those words.

All my trouble that winter was because of June. It was those rides in the walker. During race time, Grandma Corie would move her chair just out of sight by the front room doorway. As we raced to the "finish line," she would stretch her feet across the doorway. Of course, we crashed, "ka wham" right into her legs. "Lucian," she would yell. "Get in here right now. These bad girls are running into my legs again."

Since June was just along for the ride; I was the "bad girl" in trouble. Daddy would sit me down and begin his talk, "You know you're not supposed to run into Grandma Corie"—I had to interrupt—"but Daddy, she puts her legs out. I can't miss them. It's not my fault."

Usually the punishment was that I had to say, "I'm sorry." I hated that part because I knew I had to say it, but I really wasn't sorry. No one seemed to care that this wasn't my fault.

Daddy pushed June into the kitchen where she was given a cookie while she watched Mama getting supper. I had to sit very quietly on a chair with no cookie. Sometimes I got to read a book while sitting. Usually not! The worst part was that I had to sit in the front room where Grandma Corie sat, just looking at me and smiling the whole time. It was not the happiest of times, I think, not for any of us—not even Grandma Corie. For that I **am** sorry. But spring finally came; we had made it through.

Everyone looked forward to the Sinclair sponsored family gatherings. Three or four times during the year, a company dance was held in the Armory building in Seminole. Just about every one from the lease would go—Moms, Dads, and all the kids.

I remember there was usually a western swing band with a girl singer. Some of the people would dance, but everyone seemed to have a good time visiting and being together. Before the evening ended, someone was sure to call for a jig dance. The fiddles and guitar would warm up and then go into a jigging song. Champion jig dancer was Whitey Seifried—Mabel's father. He was a tiny man and his feet could fly. Sometimes he would challenge Daddy to a "jig down." The fiddlers' hands were a blur as the music heated up. Whitey and Daddy put in a few fancy steps as their feet moved faster and faster.

I liked to slip into the shadows and try a little "jigging" myself. Of course, I just stomped around, but I thought I did really good. Well, not quite good enough to get out on the dance floor where someone might see.

At last, Daddy would laugh as he headed for a chair, "Well, Whitey, you got me bested again."

"But, Pat, you sure 'nuff gave it a shot," Whitey would say. "Guess we'd better have a little drink. (Oklahoma was a prohibition state in those days, so the "drink" was pop or lemonade.)

The biggest Sinclair party was always the Fourth of July picnic at Wewoka Lake. It was an all-day celebration with swimming, games, food and ended with fireworks at night. Everyone on the lease looked forward to this day. I loved every single minute of it.

There were so many things to do, but I knew where I wanted to start. As soon as we parked, I grabbed Daddy's hand. "Come on, Daddy, push me in the swing. Please! Please!" These swings were on pipe frames and the chains on each side of the seat stretched upward forever. At first, the swing went back and forth at an easy pace, but soon, I was calling out, "Push me higher, Daddy! Higher!" When he gave an extra shove, Mama, watching from under a shade tree, would caution, "Now, Lucian, that's high enough!" But it wasn't. I wanted to be able to stretch out my foot and touch the waving leaves in the tree branches above the swings.

"Higher, Daddy! Higher!" Finally, I reached as far as I could and grazed the leaves with the tips of my toes. I dared not look down; I just kept my face turned up to the sky. I was flying. "That's enough now, let's walk around and see who else is here." said Mama.

Gradually my "plane" slowed and finally came to a stop. As I slide off the seat and looked up, I could see the tree branches. "Oh my gosh! Had I really been way up there?"

As we left the playground, I grabbed Daddy's hand. "Let's go ride the Dodgems, OK?" These electric-powered bumper cars rolled around on a wooden rink. The object was to hit someone else's car with your bumper car, while avoiding getting hit. Of course, if you hit another car, that meant your car got hit too. That's something I didn't think of then..

I was too little to ride by myself, so Daddy used two of our tickets— one for me and one for him to be my co-pilot. He did let me steer a little, but we usually ended up in a traffic jam going nowhere. Even though the ride lasted for a quite a while, it seemed too short for me.

By the time we came off the Dodgem rink, Mama was more than ready to find some other people from the lease. Daddy went off to play horseshoes while Mama, June and I headed for the beach. She put June down in the sand and settled herself for a little talk with the other Mamas from the lease.

All of us kids were ready for a swim. Mabel had taken on the job of looking after us. We jumped into the water to cool off, then ran right out again. Most of us settled down on the beach to build elaborate sand castles at the lake's edge. We spent a lot of time on them adding spires and moats, and protecting them from any other kids who wanted to stomp them down. On this beach, Tornado's Comin' was a game not allowed.

But enough was enough. Someone called out, "Let's eat!" It didn't take a second call to get us headed for the picnic area. We were more than ready for the feast provided by Sinclair (or as Daddy so fondly said, "Uncle Harry.")

The hot dogs dripped mustard and the corn-on-the-cob dripped butter. I'm sure there were other things just as tasty, but I liked the messy stuff. I passed up cake for the juicy red watermelon slices that ran down my elbows to mix with the mustard and butter that was all over my clothes. Later I would put on the "change of clothes for when I got dirty" that Mama always brought for me. She said it was to keep the flies from carrying me away.

Finally evening came and as the sky began to darken, we all went down to the beach and found seats on the bleachers to wait for the fireworks display. Across the lake we could see the men scurrying around getting ready to dazzle our eyes with beauty.

Just when I started to squirm around and think they were never going to begin, there was a whooshing sound followed by a sudden burst of color. All eyes turned to the sky where the first skyrockets lit up the night. With loud explosions, others rockets burst, then ran down in rainbows of reds and greens and blues and gold. "Look at that!" The crowd responded with gasps of appreciation. Surely nothing had ever been so beautiful. It was like a million Roman candles shooting out in all directions.

After awhile, the crowd grew quiet. The sky grew dark again. Across the lake we could see men working around a huge frame set up at the very edge of the water. As they touched the lighting torches to the bottom edges, red, white and blue began to climb upward, until there before our eyes the American flag appeared to be ruffling in the breeze.

Someone began the singing, "Oh, beautiful, for spacious skies." Others joined in and by the time they reached "From sea to shining sea" every person was singing. I will never forget the sight and sound of that display, and to this day, my heart is full to running over with the glory of the evening.

Gradually, the flag would begin to drift downward in a shower of color. I didn't know it then, but one day I would look at the magnificent Niagara Falls, and think of that flag across Wewoka Lake and how it appeared to shower into the water.

Mama always missed her Illinois family the most at Thanksgiving time, so she looked forward to the "lease" Thanksgivings under the hill. All the people of the lease who didn't have local family would gather at the Seifrieds for the holiday. Often there would be as many as sixty people with each family bringing something to add to the overflowing table.

Mrs. Seifried would always tend the turkey, with yummy cornbread dressing. But I think her real talent was in making pies. She would fill the table on the closed-in back porch with pies—pecan, pumpkin, persimmon, cherry, apple, mincemeat and many other kinds. I made it a point to walk by as often as possible, and sometimes, if no one was around, I would sneak a pecan or a little taste of one or another.

After dinner, while the "old folks" settled down for a little nap, we kids would take a walk. This usually led to the thicket where we would pick up pecans and hickory nuts. The nut trees were at the edge, so no one really went into the thicket. Someone would mention the goat man, but no one really wanted to track him down—least of all me. Some claimed to have seen him at one time or another, but this was one time I kept my mouth shut. When we started home with our nuts and a few persimmons, I never looked back.

We went back to our shotgun houses Thanksgiving evening with a feeling of thankfulness—for having our own families and the families of the lease.

In the early fall of 1937, my third year in school, Daddy came home from work with an announcement, "It looks like we're moving again."

"What do you mean, moving? Moving where? Is there a house? Why are we doing this again?"

"Yes, we have a house on the lease at Sinclair Plant 14. The place is called Saint Louis and it's about 20 miles from here. You'll like it, Toots. The Cherry Hill school is right across the road from our house. You can walk to school. I have to be there Monday morning." How could he know if I would like it or not? But Daddy was usually right, so I didn't say anything more.

Surprisingly, Mama didn't say much, and the next day I helped her wrap the dishes with dishrags and newspapers and put them in boxes. I told my friend, Norma Jean, we were moving, and we said good bye to the Seifrieds and other families of the lease.

"St. Louis isn't far," they said. "Ya'll will come over. We'll see each other all the time." But we didn't, except for the Seifrieds and the Davises, we seldom saw any of them again. We did go back for Thanksgiving that year, and it was fun, but for some reason, not quite the same as before.

Moving day came and as we headed west, I wondered what the new school would be like. How many rooms would the house have? Would I have a real bed this time? What would my new friends be like? I guessed I would find out soon enough.

Little did I know that this was the move that would take me "truly home."

PART THREE

Cherry Hill

Route 59 cuts a path southwest through the country from Seminole to Saint Louis and in those days as soon as we turned west off Highway 99, the dust began to fly and rocks banged against the fenders. The trailer hooked on behind us bounced around like popcorn in a hot skillet.

"Good lands," said Mama as she wiped her face with a hanky. "I've never seen it this hot for October." My eyes were filled with red dust as I tried to see where we were going. I needn't have bothered, 'cause I sure wasn't seeing anything new. Only the usual Oklahoma countryside— red fields cut with gullies, an occasional creek with a few willow trees and lots of brush filtered through the dust. A few cows were grazing on the brown grass.

"This doesn't look like much to me!" I thought, but I kept quiet. As usual, Mama didn't keep quiet. She didn't sound too happy either, "Well, it looks like we're on our way to the edge of nowhere—again."

"Aw, Spanky, cheer up. Here's a town. Let's take a look," said Daddy as he turned onto a blacktopped street. The sign read, "Maud." We passed a couple of grocery stores. Daddy sounded like a tour guide. "I bet that dry goods store will have some material you'll like, Thelm'. Toots, that's the Arcadia picture show. We can see some "whoop it up" Saturday night cowboys, just like the Rialto at Seminole. We'll sure give it a try." I thought he was trying too hard to sound excited.

"Humph," scowled Mama, "some big town. Must be at least three blocks long." I did notice that she snuck a look toward the dry goods store.

"Hey, there's a drug store with an ice cream sign. Can we stop and get an ice cream cone?" June perked up a little. Ice cream was a word she knew.

Mama sniffed, "We don't have time for ice cream. We've got to have a place to sleep settled in by bedtime."

I looked out the dusty back window. The ice cream sign disappeared behind us as Daddy turned back onto the graveled road. He began to whistle, "Bringin' in the Sheaves," and before long, we were all singing.

As we left Maud behind, I saw a few oil wells scattered around the fields. We came to a crossroads with a couple of filling stations and a McGuffeys' General Store with another ice cream sign. Daddy slowed a little and I thought, "Oh, I bet he's gonna get ice cream here."

But it didn't happen. Instead he turned onto a red clay washboard road. I tried to hold on to June and the boxes in the seat as we bounced up and down and side to side. I wondered, "Is this really a road?"

"Hang on, Toots, we're nearly there," Daddy said. One more mile, and we came to another crossroads with two more grocery stores and more houses. I could see a schoolhouse and just across a gully creek was a gasoline plant. "Must be plant 14," I thought. One more turn and Daddy pulled across a cattle guard and stopped.

As he shut off the car, he turned to us and said, "Well, this is it. This is Cherry Hill. There's your school, Toots, just like I promised. Right across the road. Over yonder is the plant. I can walk to work. What do ya' think, Spanky?"

Mama didn't say anything. She was looking at the house and she seemed surprised. I was looking, too, and for sure, I was surprised. I couldn't believe my eyes! It was a painted house—a white, painted shotgun house! We hadn't lived in a painted house since we left Grandma's.

As Daddy opened the front door I ducked under his arm and ran inside. There was our furniture and boxes all jammed together. I didn't know how they got there, but, sure enough, that was our couch; so that meant my bed was here. I wouldn't be sleeping on the floor tonight.

I ran into the kitchen and saw a closed door. "Hm—wonder what that could be?" When I opened the door, there it was—a bathroom! A real, inside bathroom! I could only think, "Mama and Daddy must be really rich! First a painted house and now a bathroom."

Beyond the kitchen was a kind of closed in porch and I figured this must be Mama and Daddy's bedroom, because June's bed was there already put together.

I ran back to the kitchen, where I checked out that bathroom one more time. "Hey, Mama, can we really use this bathroom. I'm really hot and all dusty. Could I try out this tub now?"

"No time now. I've got jobs for everybody." Soon Mama had each one of us doing something. By bedtime, she had accomplished her goal, a place for everyone to sleep with clean sheets on the beds.

She made some sandwiches and cut the Lazy-Dazy cake some lady had dropped off. "Maybe this place won't be so bad after all."

We sat around the table, but before we ate, Daddy returned thanks for the food, for the safe move, for the new friends we would make, and for our first night in Cherry Hill.

As I snuggled down into my familiar bed, I wondered what it would be like here. It seemed to me that we moved often, but I remembered Daddy always said, "It's gonna be OK," so I guess it was up to me to give

Mildred Dennis

it a chance. It was comforting to hear the old familiar pump-chug-pump sound in the distance—my lease lullabies were still there, as constant as my life.

THOSE WHO CAME BEFORE

After talking with many of the Saint Louis/Cherry Hill alumni, I've concluded that most of us feel the same about this place where we grew up. Our lives were shaped significantly by those early men and women who had the courage and fortitude to settle what was then a part of Indian Territory. The kids of my generation attended school and were friends with their grandchildren. We even knew some of these pioneers personally. It seems to be only fitting to honor them by remembering how it all started.

. . . "And God called the dry land Earth; and the gathering together of the waters He called seas; and God saw that it was good." Genesis 1:10

And that part of the Earth that became the greater Saint Louis area stayed unchanged for thousands of years, but deep beneath the surface of the red dirt, subtle changes were taking place. At different depths, rivers of oil were beginning to flow.

When this area of Indian Territory was opened for settlement in September, 1891, as a part of the Potawatomi and Shawnee Indian lands, it was considered to be a very poor risk for economic development. Not many people wanted to establish claims, so most of the land to the southwest of Maud was left to the coyotes and horny toads.

As Washington Irving explored the land south of Oklahoma City in 1832, he wrote of a distinctive line between the prairie on the right and the area to the left which he called "Cross Timbers." Black jack and post-oak trees covered the red dirt gullies and gently rolling hills. A few black walnut and native pecan trees were scattered around, but grassland was very limited.

Finally, a few farmers who had become disenchanted with their lot in Arkansas and Texas began to arrive. Moving a family was a very difficult undertaking, but these were hardy men and women. They were looking for permanent homes, a place to become one with the land.

One of the earliest to come was Ivy Tarter. In 1889, he brought his wife and children from Texas and settled just north of the (Hilton) crossroads. His closed-in front porch served as a post office from 1903 to 1905. The place was called Sillar (Cillar) named for Ivy's daughter. He also gave an acre of land for a school.

J. R. and Molly Simpson also came up from Texas around 1890. They settled their thirteen children on a farm just south of Pop City. On land which he owned north of the "crossroads," J. R. built a cotton gin and a general store around 1900. In 1906, he added a grist mill. The "crossroads" came to be known as The Store, but before long people began calling the place Simpsonville, and this name became official with statehood on November 7, 1907. Later, Simpson sold his store and cotton gin to W. S. Carson, who made several improvements.

Farming flourished with crops of cotton, corn and a little tobacco. New settlers came by wagons and trains from Arkansas and Texas.

In 1902, Benjamin M. Green, a Primitive Baptist minister, with only a wagon and a one-horse buggy, started the long haul from Arkansas to Indian Territory. He brought his wife and six children and all his belongings and settled on 160 acres north of Pop City. In addition to preaching, he farmed, traded in hides, dealt in real estate and in 1910, he opened the area's second grist mill.

W. H. Hilton chose to bring his family (wife and four children) by train from Arkansas in 1905. Freight cars carried their furniture, wagon, farm equipment, cattle and a team of horses. They unloaded at Romulus depot and headed south.

It was the job of two sons, Robert (age 10) and Guy (age 8) to drive the cattle to the new farm. The boys got lost, but by chance came to the Green farm where they waited for the rest of the family.

A few years later, Grace Hilton and John Little Green were married; thus, joining two of the Saint Louis pioneer families.

W. H. farmed for a few years, and in 1919, he purchased the Robbins General Store and Hilton and Sons General Store came into existence. For 25 years, the store provided everything from groceries to banking to dry goods and feed for the local people. For a while, it served as a mail drop for area residents. It wasn't a "real" post office; just a service offered by Hiltons Store

The store was sold to Floyd Fowler in 1944, and, with various owners, provided continuous service for almost 100 years. Peggy and Paul Wayne Allen were the final owners. Peggy offered basic supplies and lunch to local residents and workers until April, 2004.

Paul Wayne is the great grandson of Betty Patrick Milbern, who lived for a time with her husband and five children in a "dugout" just west of Cherry Hill.

No one seems to know exactly when Simpsonville became Saint Louis. Many stories of how the renaming came about have been told, but most people lean toward this version.

Samuel Gratis Johnson, a $40 per month teacher at Unity School north of Pop City, stopped to talk with a friend while walking to town. As a joke, Sam said, "Better get going. I'm on my way to that bustling town of Saint

Louis." People liked the story, and began using the name, Saint Louis, without the abbreviated spelling.

Frank Rosamond came over from Arkansas looking for the murderer of his father. For a while he slept in a barn at Ray City, got a job, and continued his search. By the time he learned that the man he was looking for had been killed in a gun fight in Southern Oklahoma, he had met and married another Sooner pioneer, Lillie. After they made their home in Saint Louis, he and Lillie felt the town should have some organization, so they plotted the town, and on March 9, 1927, they filed the official document under the name, Saint Louis.

The town and surrounding farms remained a small agricultural community until 1925. When J. M. Robbins sold 160 acres to the Magnolia Oil Company, the winds of change began to sweep across the countryside like a northerner blowing in from the Panhandle.

Darby Oil Company brought in the first Saint Louis well on July 20, 1926. But it was shallow, producing only 125 barrels a day. In the summer of 1928, T. B. Slick promised to drill the biggest well so far—and he did!

His venture at Ray City came in as a gusher with a production rate of nearly 10,000 barrels a day. Like magic, derricks appeared everywhere and the pumping sounds sang a special music to the wildcatters' ears. The greater Saint Louis area became one of the greatest oil patches in Oklahoma. Almost overnight, an area with a population of less than 1,000 burgeoned to almost 10,000 people. The oil companies brought in workers over the next couple of years to drill the wells and do all the work related to the production of oil and gas. Some of these workers were single men, but many brought families from all over the Midwest.

Two companies, Sinclair and Magnolia, built refineries that were in operation until the early seventies. Each company had its own "camp" built on land leased usually from Indian owners. (Could this be the reason they were called "leases?")

Other major companies with operations in the area were Gulf, SunRay, Pure, Phillips, Gypsy and Atlantic.

Workers and families slept in whatever place a bed could be found—shotgun houses, tents, garages, barns and even chicken houses. (Several of my friends were born and/or lived in tents during the fierce winter of 1929.) Schools, churches, and businesses of all types sprang up. In some of the boomtowns, crime was a major problem. Saint Louis seems to have escaped the worst of the crime scene, although the old jail complete with the outhouse still stands along the main road.

One thing is sure, this flow of black gold shaped the lives of all of us—those who were there when it started and those of us who came a bit later.

By the time the "Murphy's" moved into that white painted house with inside plumbing, the "boom" had become more of a rumble. Tents had turned into shotgun and company houses. Churches and schools had been built and I became a part of the more normal way of life that had taken hold in the Saint Louis/Cherry Hill area.

BACK TO THE LEASE KID

I had started third grade at Seminole before we moved. Now, the leaves were turning to gold and I felt like I was starting all over again. I know I was feeling anxious, maybe I was a little afraid to get started at the new school, but I tried not to let on.

"Mama, let's go. I don't want to be late." I smoothed down my "Sunday" dress. Mama had said I could wear it for the first day if I was careful.

"It doesn't start till nine o'clock. We have plenty of time." She took a last sip of coffee, put the cup in the sink, picked up June and said, "Well, come on. We might as well go. You know it's just across the road."

Of course I knew that. I picked my way carefully across the rocks in the road, down and up the bar ditch and through the gate into the schoolyard. As we pushed open the front door of the school, a lady met us, smiled and said, "Y'all must be the new Sinclair people from across the road. And I'll bet this young lady is ready to enroll in our school. Come this way."

She took my hand and Mama followed us down the hall. June was chattering all the way, and I whispered, "Shut up, June." She didn't but, thank goodness, Mama told her to be quiet. Then she told the lady, "This is my girl, Mildred Murphy, and she's in the third grade."

"We'll get the details later," the lady said as she stopped at the door of a room full of kids. She said it was the third and fourth grade room.

We went in and I could feel everyone looking at me. The lady introduced Mama to the teacher and while they talked, I looked around. I saw no Sunday School dresses—just overalls and plain everyday dresses.

I slipped behind Mama, but the teacher took my hand and led me to an empty seat. I think she knew I was a little scared. "Mildred," she smiled, "I'm Miss Ivey. You can sit here beside Roella. Her daddy works at the plant, too."

Somehow I squeaked out a tiny, "Hi." Roella smiled, but didn't say anything.

My first day at the Cherry Hill school had begun!

I sat still and watched what was going on. There was a reading circle. Some other kids were writing spelling words on the board and a few were making pushpulls and ovals on penmanship paper. The teacher moved from group to group. A couple of the older girls seemed to be helping. I didn't do anything—just watched. Um-m, this didn't seem too strange.

One of the girls was dressed-up. She looked like a Shirley Temple doll with her long golden curls. Seemed like she talked a lot, too. I heard the teacher call her "Bonnie Jean."

When it was time for recess, the teacher came over and suggested, "I'm sure Roella would like to show you the rest of the school." "OK," I said, "If she wants to." (Roella has remained a special friend for the past 67 years.)

We walked through the big hallway down the middle of the building. "There's the first/second grade room next to ours," Roella pointed out. On the other side was the fifth/sixth room and another big room with tables and chairs and a stage. "We eat lunch in here and have programs and do lots of other stuff," said Roella.

Outside she pointed to two outhouses, with covered entryways. "That's the girls' toilet, and over there is the boys'. Miss Ivey doesn't like it much if we have to go out during class."

I saw swings and a slide and a merry-go-round. I looked around at the kids playing games and running around. "I guess y'all do lots of different things at recess."

"See that big tree. We play house there. We do have a pretty good time. Uh oh, there's the bell. We'd better go back in now. The teacher doesn't like for us to be late."

I felt a little better after recess, and sat in a reading circle. I just listened to the others; I didn't want to read yet. When lunchtime came, Roella asked me to eat with her, but I didn't have a lunch at school. Mama had told me to come home.

I ran across the road, and didn't care if the screen door slammed behind me. "Mama, I need my lunch bucket. The kids at this school bring their lunches, just like in Seminole. I don't want to come home to eat. I need to change my dress. They wear just plain ole clothes, not Sunday School clothes. Some even have on overalls."

Mama had a bowl of soup steaming on the table. "You'll have to eat here today, so sit down and get started. You don't want to be late for this afternoon." She gave a big sigh, "and you don't have time to change your dress today."

As I slouched down in the chair, I complained, "This soup is too hot. How can I hurry?" But somehow I got it down and ran back to school.

That evening Daddy asked, "How was school today, Toots?" Before I even thought about it, I heard "his words" coming out of my mouth, "It's gonna be OK."

He laughed at me. "You think so, huh?"

And before I knew it, we were both right. It was OK. I became one of the Cherry Hill lease kids, just like everybody else.

Many of our school activities were centered around holidays. Thanksgiving was coming up next. We cut out black Pilgrim hats and made Indian headbands. It was the custom to have a play or an operetta remembering the Pilgrims. The kids' Mamas and Daddies came bringing cookies and pumpkin pies and other good things to eat.

We decorated the assembly room with dry corn shocks and a few pumpkins. The play for this year was "The Courtship of Miles Standish." John Alden and Priscilla Mullin were the other main characters, and several Pilgrims and Indians had parts standing around. The characters had been chosen before I came. Bonnie Jean played the part of Priscilla. (Before long, I found out that Bonnie Jean usually played the main parts in all the Cherry Hill plays.) I became a part of the "friendly" Indians group and wore my headband and construction paper feather with pride.

As Christmas approached, I really wanted to be Mary in the play. But it wasn't to be—you're right, Bonnie Jean got the part. After thinking about the different pictures I'd seen, I asked Mama, "Do you think that Mary had long golden curls?" Mama knew why I was asking this question. "Probably not," she said, "but you know, Bonnie Jean is a pretty little girl."

I wondered about her answer, "Does this mean that I'm not a pretty little girl?"

The program went well, and the big Christmas tree with its paper ornaments was beautiful. I sang in the choir and I thought our "Little Town Of Bethlehem" and "Silent Night" sounded pretty good. (By the next year, I had memorized every word of "The Night Before Christmas" and I recited it the night of the Christmas program. Everyone asked, "How did you ever memorize that whole poem?")

Right after the Christmas holidays we started getting ready for Valentine's Day. We drew names so that everyone would have at least one card. We made the Valentines in art class, but a few lucky people had "bought" valentines too. It was a treat to be chosen to help decorate the big box that would be the mailbox for the cards. When Miss Ivey chose me as one of the helpers, I could hardly wait to go home and tell Mama.

"Guess what, Mama! Hey, mama, where are you? Guess what! I get to help decorate the Valentine box this year. What do you think of that?"

"Sh-shush! Don't wake up your sister. I thought I would never get her down this afternoon," whispered Mama.

"But, Mama, what do you think?"

"Well, of course, that's nice. Now run outside and play."

I went outside being very, very careful not to slam the door. I wanted to think of all the ways we could fix the box to make it the best one ever.

"Sometimes things go just right!" I thought.

We celebrated all the other spring holidays: Lincoln and Washington's birthdays, Saint Patrick's Day, Easter and some that I'd never heard of.

On May 1, we had a big celebration outside. I don't know the history of the holiday, but we called it May Pole Day. We tied crepe paper ribbons and streamers to a pole and danced around it while tossing the usual construction paper flowers.

The "May Pole" queen—guess who—ruled over the festivities wearing a tin foil-covered cardboard crown and waving her royal scepter. I liked dancing around the pole, so I didn't care who was queen.

We had games and races and, of course, refreshments.

My favorite May Day activity was the basket surprises. We folded and cut construction paper to make baskets that looked like Japanese lanterns and filled them with flowers. I always made one for Mama and for Mrs. Elliott, the plant superintendent's wife. She and Mr. Elliott had no kids to make a basket.

The idea was to hang the basket of flowers on the front door knob, bang on the door, yell "Surprise," then run and hide. Hopefully the person would come to the door and find the flowers. Mama would act real surprised and pleased to find the flowers. She always said, "Well, my goodness, just lookee here. I wonder where in the world these came from. I sure wish I knew who to thank."

She would take them in and put a glass of water in the basket if the flowers were real. She knew where they came from, and I knew that, but we pretended she didn't know. I was glad that she liked them.

I passed this custom on to my daughter, and on May 1, I would hear myself saying, "My goodness, just lookee here. I wonder where in the world these came from. I sure would like to thank that person." May baskets still give me a reason to smile.

We did a lot of "playing" at Cherry Hill, but the playing was very much connected to learning. We had spell downs, arithmetic contests, reading circles, covered pages and pages of penmanship papers and still had time for history—especially about Oklahoma.

In the spring, we went to the district contests at Shawnee. I don't remember how we did every time, but I do remember hall bulletin boards covered with certificates.

It was a special honor to be chosen to sing in the Cherry Hill girls' glee club, which included girls from grades three through six. I was ready to pop when I rushed home to tell Mama, "Guess what, I've been chosen to sing in the glee club. Can you make me a dress before contest time?" The dresses were blue dotted Swiss with a little white bow at the collar. I thought they were beautiful and, of course, Mama did get my dress finished in plenty of time.

Did we win? Sometimes, but the real fun was getting to go to all the different places to sing. One time we went all the way to Ada on the school bus to sing at the College there. What an experience!

Recess at Cherry Hill could be risky, always rough and tumble. The older kids were the leaders and chose up sides to play ball, or Red Rover, or Crack the Whip. If I was chosen for one of these games, I spent more time on the ground than playing. I was small and a perfect target for the bigger kids to knock over and score points. Also, spending time on the ground meant getting dirty. That didn't score many points at home.

Some of us played jump rope, or hopscotch, or jacks (my favorite). Funny how your favorite is usually what you do best. We swept the red dirt under the big tree with weed brooms, marked off rooms and played house.

Our game of "tag" had a different twist. The girl who was "It" had to grab some boy's cap and throw it over the entrance to the girls' toilet. There were two reasons for grabbing the cap: one was because you really liked the boy; the other was because you really DIDN'T like the boy. Paul lost his hat a lot because most of the girls really didn't like him much. He could be mean and he didn't seem to like anybody—girl or boy. The other problem was he would just walk into the entrance, get his cap and shout, "Y'all better watch out! I'm going to look in the door of your toilet!"

This would start all the girls screaming, even if we weren't inside. Some tattletale would always run to tell the teacher, which meant Paul and the girls were in trouble. I've sometimes wondered why we bothered with his cap anyway.

Was Cherry Hill a model for most "lease schools" in the late '30's? I'm not sure, but it became my school and I really liked it.

Holidays were always special for our family, but I think Christmas was probably the best one of all at our house. Daddy never knew much of a Christmas celebration when he was a little boy, so it was as if he were making up for that lost time.

Decorating the big tree was a family affair. Daddy would put together strings of lights of all shapes. His favorites were the Japanese lanterns and one shaped like a jolly Santa Claus. Mama's specialty was the icicles. They were the last decoration and had to be put on "just so" one at a time. Mama would give a few icicles to June and me and show us how to lay them very carefully across the branches. Daddy would stand back, grab a handful and throw a bunch all at once.

He was so anxious to turn on the lights, but Mama really fussed, "Lucian, you're worse than these girls. If you can't put them on right, then just let us do it," and she would snatch the icicles out of his hands. Finally, she would give the O.K. "Plug 'em in." He would plug in the lights and we would sit and look at our beautiful tree for awhile. Without fail, Daddy would say, "Yep, it's the best tree ever." Of course, we all agreed.

As the days moved on toward Christmas, packages would appear under the tree. Daddy would say, "Looks like the elves were busy again last night." I knew "who had been busy." But I never let on as I laughed, "Yep, I guess they were."

It was always a big day when the Illinois package arrived filled with smaller packages for each of us. When no one was looking, June and I would sit under the tree and shake some of them. We would try to guess what could be inside. If Mama came in, we would pretend we were putting an ornament back on the tree.

Christmas Eve was our special time. Traditionally Mama fixed potato soup for supper along with her own dill pickles. She'd say, "I'll be cookin' all day tomorrow, so this is it for tonight." I thought Mama's potato soup was really good; I'm pretty sure she thought so too.

After supper, we would turn on the tree lights and sit together while we read the Christmas story from Luke. After I learned to read, Daddy would let me read about how Jesus was born in Bethlehem. Then we would sing Jingle Bells and Silent Night.

Finally, when Daddy could stand it no longer, he would say, "Let's open the packages." Some were carefully wrapped in pretty paper. Others were brown paper bags with our names—mine had "Toots!" scrawled across the front. These were little surprises that Daddy had bought—a pair of socks or a hair ribbon or something like that. After the packages, it was time for popcorn balls. Mrs. Elliott made them by the bagsful and on Christmas Eve Day, she delivered them to all the Sinclair camp kids. Over the years she must have made hundreds and they were SO good!

One Christmas I got a big, big surprise—a pair of roller skates and a red wagon. I had so wanted both, but wasn't sure I would get even one— let alone both.

For June, Santa had left a doll buggy and a big baby doll waiting for a ride. Both of us were happy. I was trying to adjust my skates and in her "Dutchy" way, June was singing to her baby,

A big concrete slab on the corner was all that was left of an oilfield supply building. It was perfect for our neighborhood skating rink. After school, the kids would gather at the slab. Those who had skates would skate for a while, then would share with the ones who didn't have skates. Because the metal skates were so adjustable, the sizes didn't matter that much. Till that Christmas I had been a watcher. Now I could be a skater.

Christmas day had hardly dawned, and I was pestering Daddy, "When are we going down to the corner? When can I learn to skate? You promised you would teach me."

"Not today, but soon," he said.

And, soon we did. Mama put my skate key on a ribbon to hang around my neck so I wouldn't lose it. Of course, the usual caution words followed, "Be careful. You don't want to fall and break your arm or your leg."

With Daddy's help, lots of skinned knees and elbows, and an on-going sore bottom, I did learn to skate. I spent hours on that concrete slab and it was every bit as wonderful as I had thought it would be. The first time I crossed one foot over the other to turn a corner, I thought sure I was flying.

I never did get brave enough to play tin-can hockey with the bigger kids. In fact, I stayed off the rink when that was going on; but it was fun to watch, as long as I stayed out of the way of any flying tin cans.

Saturday nights at home were always "Grand Ole Opry" or WLS Barn Dance nights. Uncle Dave Macon and Lulu Belle and Scotty were like "family." Mama would pop up a dishpan full of popcorn and we'd sit around the radio eating popcorn, listening to the music and joining in with the singing. Minnie Pearl's "Howdy" was always good for a few laughs— especially from Daddy. Sometimes he would talk back to her.

I was only a little surprised when Daddy came in from Seminole one afternoon with a big package. "Toots," he grinned, "how would you like to play the guitar?" He pulled a guitar that was almost bigger than me out of that package..

I looked at the guitar and looked at Daddy. "OK I guess, do you really think I could learn to play this thing? Who's gonna' teach me? Daddy, do you know how to play?"

"Naw," he said. But I found this guy named Paul at Maud and he gives lessons. He said he has room for you in the class and you can start next week."

I thought the day would never come. All week I'd pick up the guitar and hold it just the way I'd seen the cowgirls do it in the movies. I'd plunk the strings and June would sing with me till Mama would say in exasperation, "Stop that noise till you know what you're doing."

Finally, the day came, and Daddy and I were off to Maud. There were four or five other people in the class. Paul gave me a smile, and said he was glad I'd decided to join them. He gave me a Nick Maniloff book, a place to sit and showed me how to wrap my left hand around the neck of the guitar.

It didn't take many lessons to discover that I wasn't a child prodigy and I wasn't going to learn to do this overnight. Also, I was going to have some very sore fingertips for a long time.

But I liked the idea, and I stuck with it.

By summer, I could chord several songs, especially some of the old gospel songs and at home we would all sing together. This included June, and though her tones were OK, no one except me and Mama knew a word she was singing. June had a language all her own and needed an interpreter to be understood. No matter where we were when she shouted "Noy!" only I knew that she was calling me.

As time passed, I began to sing and play specials at church and sometimes at school assemblies. Paul had a little string band and sometimes I would chord with them over at George's Pig Stand near Maud. These were "outside performances" and most of the people sat in their cars to listen to the music. A lot of horn-honking showed approval for a particular rendition of a song. Sometimes couples would dance on the little concrete slab at the side of the building.

Not many people who came for the music went inside. Certainly not me! They sold a little 3.2 beer across the bar, so it was definitely "off-limits" for a 10-year-old, want-to-be guitar player who happened to live in a state where prohibition was the law. In retrospect, the peace between the "drinkers" inside and the "music people" outside was pretty amazing.

Mama made matching pinafores with bonnets for three-year-old June and for me, Daddy bought us cowboy boots and we "performed" for anyone who would listen. Our best duet was "Playmates." My best solos were "Old Shep," "Ridin' Down The Canyon," or maybe "Wabash Cannon Ball."

Then came our big chance for fame. Some talent scout from the WKY radio station at Oklahoma City came to Saint Louis and held a big contest at the school. The winner would win a prize, but even better, would get to perform on the radio station in the City!

"Daddy, do you think June and I could do this? Could we be in the contest? Maybe we would win!"

"Well, you sure can't win if you don't try," encouraged Daddy. "Let's get you signed up."

On the big night, I was so excited and nervous. Of course, June wasn't nervous. She just stood up there, grinning and tossing around her golden curls, then belted out words that no one could understand.

Naturally, we did our best song, "Playmates." As it turned out, the people clapped so much, we sang it twice. We won second place and did get a prize. But I confess, I was disappointed that we wouldn't be on the radio.

LaVerne Davis, who played the piano like a real master, won first place. Truthfully, he deserved it. But, by the time he was to appear on the WKY radio program, his dad had been transferred out of the state. Someone said the talent person looked for me and June, but we were on vacation. (And to think, I could have been a star.)

I continued to play and sing at churches, school assemblies, parties and just about any place else I was asked. Sometimes June sang with me; sometimes even Daddy joined in—especially when we sang the old gospel songs. I wonder if Daddy had visions of the "Murphy Trio" right up there along side the "Stamps Quartet."

Just before school started each year, folks looked forward to the Sinclair watermelon feast. In the spring, Mr. Elliott, the plant superintendent, would have the seeds planted down south at the water station. Someone cared for the patch over the summer and, come August, when it was harvest time, the melons were loaded on a truck and brought to the big open space between the company houses.

Around 50 employees and their families would gather at the company "playground" for the end-of-summer celebration. It was fun for everyone, even the ones who only sat at the tables and watched—usually with critical comments on how the games were going.

While the kids played ball and tag and had races, the grown-ups kept the croquet tournament going at a hot pace. My mama really liked to play croquet and she really hated losing. She wouldn't partner with Daddy 'cause he wouldn't take the game seriously and had too much fun. Each year there was a highly disputed championship team.

When everyone was about ready to drop, Mr. Elliott walked over to the table loaded with melons and called out, "Come on now, let's have a feast!" He would cut through the first one—so red, so sweet, so juicy, so good.

Mama always had us wear old clothes 'cause eating watermelon from the rind made a real mess. She would give her usual prediction, "The flies will carry you off for sure before I can get you home."

Almost even better than eating watermelons was the time after the sun went down and the evening wind began to cool the air. The old folks would settle down around the tables and talk about the "good ole" boom days. With Roella and some of the other kids, I would stretch out on a quilt, prop up on my elbows and listen to the tales. And what tales they were—of tent towns and hard times, freezing winters and hot summers, storms and prairie fires, but always spiced up with lots of funny memories, too. I loved listening to these stories about the early days and hated to hear the call, "Better get goin'. Thanks K.R., we had a great time."

After we got home and Mama had washed off all the watermelon juice, I would go to bed and think about the early-days stories. The sound of the pumps chugging out there in the darkness meant that everything was OK. No nightmares would gallop through my dreams, just that girl that looked a lot like me running free across the lease

As the leaves of fall began turning, there was a murmuring in the wind. Rumors began flying like the blackbirds against the morning sky.

The teachers huddled together in the hall before school. We could hear them whispering together in the lunchroom; we heard some of the words. "What do you think they are going to do? Have you thought about where you might go?"

Mamas stopped to exchange the latest rumors in the grocery store. "Have you heard anything? Like when do they plan to make the move? Some of these kids have gone to Cherry Hill their whole lives. Why put them on a bus when they can walk to school? Well, they've got to put somebody in that fancy new brick addition the WPA has been working on for nearly a year."

"Well, I don't know anything about it. I do know I'd better get home and get supper on if I want a quiet evening at our house." And that would stop the rumor talk for that time.

But the rumors kept flying and I'd had enough of them. On the way home from the store, I asked Mama, "What's everybody talkin' about? Who's moving? Not us I hope, not again!"

"No we're not moving. I don't have time to talk about it right now. I've got to get home and get these groceries put away so I can get supper. You need to practice anyway. You didn't do as well as usual on your new songs this week."

As I worked on the new chords after we got home, I thought, "I'll ask Daddy about this after he gets home from the plant. I betcha' he'll tell me." So, I did and he did.

And what he said was this. "You know, Toots, things change all the time. Because the Saint Louis school is so crowded, they're making a new addition up there. And since they had to add on, they've decided to make it a big one. There are extra rooms, so they are closing the Cherry Hill school and all the district kids will go to the same school. It's called consolidation.

"Now, Toots, get that frown off your face. I know this will be hard at first. But think about it. This could be a good thing."

"But, Daddy, how can this be a good thing?" I hurried into my questions. "My school is right across the road, and it's the best school I've ever gone to. Will I have to ride the bus now? Will I have to get up early? Will I have a new teacher? What will happen to our Cherry Hill Glee Club? And what about my friends, the ones in my room, the camp kids? They already bring some of those Saint Louis kids out here. Why don't they just keep them at Saint Louis and let us stay here? And what about???"

"All right, that's enough," Daddy shushed me with a sigh. "I know this is something you may not like, but let's think about it a little. You are in the fourth grade now, and you would go to Saint Louis in a couple of years anyway. All the other lease kids are going—your friends—everyone. And think of all the new friends you will make."

"But, Daddy, what about my teacher? I like my teacher. I don't want a new teacher. I like this teacher."

"Toots, I can't make a promise about your teacher, but I can promise you this." I held my breath because I knew it was coming; and he didn't disappoint me. He gave me a big bear hug as he whispered in my ear, "You know it's gonna be OK."

After my talk with Daddy, I ran out back and climbed the old persimmon tree. Most of the leaves had dropped. I felt as lonely as it looked. I thought about all the things Daddy had said, but I didn't find any answers. I watched the gray clouds scurry across the evening sky and wrapped my arms around me. "It will probably turn cold by morning. That's the way it is here in this ole Oklahoma—hot one day, cold the next. You never know what's gonna happen."

Time passed and school seemed to go on the same as before. One day we drove up to the "brick" school just to take a look. I wasn't going to look, but my curiosity took over. I snuck a little peek. "Well look at that. It's not even done. They're still working on it. We can't move up here." Daddy didn't answer me.

Before I could believe it, the Christmas pageant night came. The record crowd clapped and cheered, and said "It's the best pageant we've ever had." I wondered why some of the ladies had tears in their eyes. Little did I know this would be our last Cherry Hill pageant.

Some man I didn't even know got up on the stage. "Before we try these good cookies and punch, I have a few words to say. This has been a joyful night and we all know the Christmas holidays start tomorrow.

Beginning January 2 (1940), the Cherry Hill school will close. All of you students will be transferred to the fine new building at Saint Louis."

He said what a good school Cherry Hill had been, and a lot of other stuff. I don't know how many people were listening. I know I wasn't. All I could think of was, "Oh, no! The rumors were right!"

During the holidays, trucks drove into the school yard and the workers began to carry things out of the school. Some of us kids sat in the swings and on the merry-go-round and watched as they carried "our school" away. The desks and chairs and tables were loaded onto the trucks. The books and supplies were boxed and loaded. We watched as the workers kept going in and out of the doors carrying "our" stuff. I wanted to yell at them, "Stop it! Stop taking our stuff!" I didn't because they weren't going to stop. Before New Years Day, it was all over; everything was gone.

After the last truck left, we looked in the windows, but there were only empty rooms. Here and there were a few scraps of paper. I wondered if they were someone's homework. No one said much. We just turned and walked home.

On Monday, January 2, Mama packed my lunch. I was ready early cause I didn't want to miss the bus the first day. When I got on, I was a little surprised, I knew everybody. But then, why not? They all lived on the lease. Soon, we were all talking, till it was time to get off the bus and begin our first day at the Saint Louis school.

I made a happy discovery. It wasn't that bad! Several kids that I already knew were mixed in with the Cherry Hill kids. Our old desks were there, but we were sitting in brand new rooms with lots of windows. Our same teacher, Mrs. Langsford, was smiling behind her desk. The girls' restroom was right down the hall. (Nobody had told me there were inside restrooms.)

One of the best surprises was just down the hall. A sign on the door read "High School Study Hall", but for me it should have read "Door To The World." Inside, all along one wall were shelves from the floor to the ceiling filled with books. (As a high school senior, I fell off of those shelves and broke my wrist. Not one of my better moments.)

The second day of school Mrs. Langsford took our class to this wonderful library and said, "You can check out one book at a time to take home and you can keep it for two weeks. Each week we will have a library time when you can pick out what you would like to read."

My gosh, this was like Christmas all over again. All those books! How would I ever decide? I still remember my first choice—"Little Women." I read it at least three times before the two weeks were up. I became one of the March family and cried buckets of tears when Beth became so sick. I sympathized with Jo who was so determined to do things her own way and that meant she was in trouble more often than not.

Before I finished high school, I had read most of those books in that "Door To The World" room.

I soon discovered that the Saint Louis school was a lot like Cherry Hill. We celebrated all the holidays with lots of construction paper art work, and some how we still had time for learning new things and recess.

One holiday was different. On November 11, Armistice Day, all the students would follow the marching band and strutting majorettes from the school to "down town," which consisted of a couple of blocks on each side of the highway. People would come in from the leases to honor the veterans of World War I.

The band played "America The Beautiful" and a preacher and a politician gave speeches. At eleven o'clock, every one stood in silence for one minute. Then after a prayer, the band played "The Star Spangled Banner," and we marched the half mile back to school. I wondered how the first and second graders ever made it.

In February, Mama and Daddy came home from Seminole honking the horn all the way from the corner. I ran outside with June. They were driving a different car — a shiny bright green '37 Ford, a five-passenger coupe called a "club coupe." It was the closest thing we ever had to a NEW car. "Is it really, really ours?" I shouted. "You bet your boots," bragged Daddy. This time it was Mama who was smiling all over her face.

Daddy was a good shade-tree mechanic and I was his chief helper. When he said, "Toots, hand me . . ." I was supposed to anticipate which tool he needed. He treated that car like a baby and it ran as well when we sold it years later as it did the day he brought it home.

There was one very big, very scary happening with that car. One hot evening in August, we got a late start leaving on vacation for Illinois and it was already dark when we cut across Route 9 northeast of Seminole. It was a pretty good graveled road so we were rolling right along.

"What the # @ ***!" Daddy yelled as he slammed on the brakes. Too late! Mama was screaming. June and I were trying to stay in the seat.

We found ourselves in a big, car-deep hole in the middle of the road. Only the top of the car could be seen. Daddy finally got the doors open helped us get out. He got back in and gunned the engine. But, there was no moving that car. It was stuck, but good!

It wasn't a busy road, but a few people did stop. Seems the road crew had been working on Route 9 and for some reason they left this big hole with no flares or any other warning.

As some of the guys were offering ideas to move the car, we heard a sound in the distance. As it came closer, it sounded a little like a train, but there was no train track. We saw headlights moving fast. Everyone started to scatter.

I couldn't move. I was down in the hole by the back of our car, hypnotized by the two lights coming toward me. Mama was already holding June in her arms, but somehow she managed to grab my arm. "Mildred, get out of here. We're gonna get killed!"

I don't know how she did it, but Mama, with June and me, hit the ditch across the road just as the roaring car hit the top of our car. Everyone was screaming, but no one louder than me. I couldn't stop!

The thunderous crash was followed by a thud and the sound of a horn that wouldn't stop honking.

It seemed as if the whole world was shaking. Gravel flew everywhere. When the dust settled, a car was crashed against the bar ditch across from the big hole. It had bounced off the top of our car, hit the other side of the hole in the road, and then hurled on across the road branching off Route 9. Luckily, except for a split lip, neither of the teenage boys seemed to be hurt. None of the other people had been hit either.

Finally, after a lot of talking, some shouting, and blaming, a farmer brought his tractor and pulled our car out of the hole. It started and seemed to run OK, but the whole top was smashed in. As far as I know the police were never called. Maybe there weren't any out on that lonely road. By then, it was after midnight.

"What are we gonna do now?" Mama cried.

"What are we gonna do?" growled Daddy. "Well, I'll tell you, the good Lord willin' and the creek don't rise, we're going to go on vacation. THAT'S WHAT we started out to do and that's what we're gonna do and don't worry, everything's gonna be O.K." Daddy was pretty agitated.

Some way he got the doors open again, put us in the car, said thanks to the people still standing around, and we headed for Illinois. Two days later, we pulled into my grandma's front yard. Of course, everyone had to look the car over. "It's just a miracle," they said, "that you weren't all killed." After riding in that smashed-in car for 700 miles with everybody staring at us, I was thinking they were probably right. I know one thing for sure; the Mickey Mouse nightmares revisited my nights for awhile, only this time his eyes were like bright headlights racing toward me.

Daddy found someone who could fix the car and the relatives shared their cars while we were there. Two weeks later, we headed home with all the damage repaired and a shiny new paint job—green, just like before.

Family Album

Author with three of Fannie's "bears."

Ugly brown stockings, even with holes, are useful in a rare Oklahoma snowfall.

Birthday party (seven years old)

Front row, Joan Gilkey, Author

Back row, Mabel

The Sailor Dress—Sister June and Author

The Murphy family on vacation—1937

The Singing Sisters (Cherry Hill school in the background)

Cherry Hill Girls' Glee Club

Front row, left, Author; Second, Bonnie Jean;

Second row, fifth from left, Roella

Cousin Maurice, Author and Trixie—Ready for vacation adventures

The beautiful, red bicycle and Author (wearing the ugly glasses).

Senior-year Basketball Team, End right, Author, Coach Mrs. Womack

Author and friend swimming in the Washita River

Author in "The Swing" with June's dog, Flossie. The green '37 Ford in background.

February 3, 1952, James and Mildred's wedding day

Daddy and Chipper, Spring, 1952

Right after we got home, Mama looked over the dried-out garden and declared, "It's time to put up the end-of-the-garden soup. I want to get it done before school starts."

I knew what that meant—a hot, all-day job and I would help.

Early the next morning, we started pulling up the plants. Beans, okra, tomatoes, a few onions and carrots and anything else left over. One thing never found in Mama's garden was blackeyed peas. In Illinois they were called "cow peas" and Mama said she did not eat cow feed. (I learned to like them, but even now she turns up her nose when I put them on my table.)

After clearing the garden, we got the vegetables snapped or shelled, washed and cut up and they were ready for the Mason jars. Mama had a brand new pressure cooker and she was anxious to try it out. It was supposed to make the canning job a lot easier.

Daddy had told her, "Wait till I get home from work and I'll help you. This first batch could be a little tricky."

Mama wasn't one to wait around. We had the jars all filled, and she sent June and me outside. She didn't have to tell me twice. It was quite awhile later that I went in to get a drink of water and check on Mama and her new pressure cooker

What a mess! Mama was sitting at the kitchen table with her face about the color of the beets we'd pulled up earlier. There was glass all over the kitchen floor and the top was off the new cooker. Mama looked like she'd been crying.

I ran over to her. "Mama, what happened? Are you O.K.?"

"Watch out where you walk," snapped Mama. "You'll cut your foot on that glass. Your Dad's gonna kill me."

"But, Mama, what happened? Are you O.K.?"

"Yes, I'm O.K. That damn pressure cooker blew up. Just look at that!" She pointed upward.

I figured this was no time to comment on the "bad" word. Instead I looked up at the ceiling. Hanging down in great globs were beans and okra, tomatoes and onions. As I think back on the sight, I would have to say our ceiling would have made a great Picasso painting. Right then, I couldn't say anything and that was probably for the best. In fact, I went back outside and stayed till after Daddy came home. Even then June and I didn't go in until Daddy called us for supper.

The glass was gone off the floor, the pressure cooker was in the sink, and although there were plenty of splotches, Picasso's painting wasn't dripping off the ceiling. It was a very quiet supper.

As time passed, Mama learned how to use the cooker, and sometimes we laughed about the great end-of-garden soup-canning episode. At least Daddy and June and I laughed. Mama didn't often join in the fun.

I was quite happy that year with the fifth grade at St. Louis. The teacher started something new. Almost every Friday afternoon at the end of the day she had a "Let's tell a story" time. Sometimes she would choose someone; other times the kids would choose.

Sometimes the teacher would tell us what the story should be about. Other times we could pick out a topic. I was excited when I was chosen and whatever the topic, I found it was great fun to tell stories. The kids liked my stories and I was chosen often. And so it was that I became a "storyteller."

It's still exciting to watch the kids eyes light up at children's church, or to coax a smile from a nursing home resident as I share a story with them.

Still, I didn't forget about my days at Cherry Hill. How could I? The building still sat straight across the road, and we lease kids often played in the yard on the swings and merry-go-round. There were new rumors that the building was to be moved to the Saint Louis school grounds. I didn't see how they could ever move a building that big.

Only a couple of years later that's exactly what happened. The building was cut straight down the middle, loaded onto two big oil field trucks and moved the two miles to Saint Louis. One side became a lunchroom. For the first time those great government "hot lunches" were served, complete with plenty of peanut butter and cheese. Actually, for ten cents the cooks served up a pretty good dinner. A few years later my mama became known as "the pie lady," when she got a job at the school making pies. All the kids were happy 'cause Mama could make really good pies.

Just after the end of school, I was sitting in the persimmon tree with the usual book in my hands. The sun's rays were shut out by the leaves and I settled down on my favorite branch. Earlier Harold Ray asked if I wanted to go down to the creek and build Indian cliff dwellings in the steep red clay sides.

"Naw," I said. "I'm gonna read my book." He headed for the creek and I climbed my tree. But I didn't pick up the book. I just sat there, feeling the wind on my face and looking at that bluest sky ever. Then a thought came to me. "I think I want to be baptized."

This was a very big thought. At first, it seemed it had just popped into my head out of nowhere. But I know now, as I knew then, that wasn't true The idea had been roaming around in my head for awhile.

My family had always gone to Sunday School and church. We often had group Bible reading and prayer study at our house. Dozens of times we would start to read the Bible through. We usually bogged down at the "begets" chapters and stopped. Sometimes we would start with the New Testament (which I liked better). Sometimes we would read in Revelations, and Daddy would explain about prophecy and the Russian bear and the Anti-Christ. I tried not to listen much because it all sounded too scary to me.

My grandfather had helped build the Church of God of the Abrahamic Faith in Illinois and we attended that small family church till we moved to Oklahoma. It sat in the middle of a cornfield at the end of a gravel lane lined with cedar trees. For a long time, I thought the road to heaven led up a lane lined with cedar trees. At the end of the lane sat this old, old person with a long white beard. It was God, and, to be honest, He scared me to death.

Jesus was a whole different story. He was my friend, He listened to my prayers, and He loved me "no matter what, even when I said 'darn' which Aunt Lizzie said was a 'hell-fire' word."

When we moved to Saint Louis I asked Daddy what church we were going to this time. There were several to choose from: the Baptist, the Methodist, the Church of Christ, the Pentacostal, the Assembly of God and a few others came and went. The Sacred Heart Mission and Indian School was down the road toward Konawa. Summer always brought a few brush arbor revivals.

The early settlers of the area had felt the need for God's presence. Often the early schools served as meeting places until churches could be built.

Daddy chose an Advent Christian Church down south by Avoca for us. Because of the distance, we usually went on Sunday morning, took a picnic dinner and stayed for evening service. Other members did the same, so Sundays were special. During the time between services, we had dinner together, played games and had singing contests. I seem to remember some very pungent Sunday evening services.

A lot of the kids went to the Baptist Bible School in the summer. No matter what name was on the front of the church, beliefs in this oil community were strong. No school activities were scheduled on Sunday and Wednesday nights were for prayer meetings.

So with this foundation, I decided that day in the persimmon tree, "It's time to confess my sins and be baptized."

That night I told Mama and Daddy. "Toots, are you sure this is what you want to do. I know we've talked about this, but do you understand what baptism is all about? Do you have questions?"

"Nope. I'm ready. Is there a Church of God preacher around who can do this?" I knew I wanted to join the church Mama and Daddy belonged to.

"I think Brother Morgan is holding a meeting later this month in Bristow. It's quite a ways, but I'll see what I can find out. Unless you want to wait until vacation later this summer."

"Nope. I'm ready."

A few weeks later, Daddy said we could go to Bristow the next Sunday and Brother Morgan would baptize me if I still wanted to do that.

"I'm sure," I said. Sunday morning we got up early and left. On the way, I thought about the Passion Play we had seen in Seminole in the spring. I remembered the face of the young man (Josef Meier). He seemed so sad, even when the people waved the branches and called out, "Hosanna!" Later when they hit Jesus, I couldn't stop the tears. When they nailed Him on the cross and lifted it up in the air, I shut my eyes as tight as I could. But I couldn't shut out the sound of His voice. "Oh, Father, why have you forsaken me?"

"Daddy, why did they do those awful things to Jesus? He loves us. I know he does!"

"You're right, He does love us and that's why He went to the cross. You will understand it better when you are older. For now, just remember that He does love you."

I'm not sure I really understand the answer to my question even now. Oh, I understand the theological answers, but my heart still wonders, "Why did my friend have to suffer so? Why did He have to die?" (It seems fateful to me that many years after my baptism, we were in Spearfish, SD and there was a billboard of this man—Joseph Meier—who had so impacted my life. Here he was 45 years later, still portraying the passion of Christ.)

About three hours later we reached Bristow. Brother Morgan and I talked for a while and I assured him I was ready. "Then let's go, young lady. I've arranged to use the local swimming pool for the service."

At the pool, the people who were swimming got out and sat along the sides. Brother Morgan and I waded into the pool; everyone was very quiet. He asked me some questions, then covered my nose, pushed me under the water and I came up baptized. We sang "Washed In The Blood" and some of the swimmers joined in.

Brother Morgan said he would send my certificate. Daddy gave him some money, and we left for home. I thought about what had happened and I felt good about it. I thought, "It will be easy to be good now. I'm sure I will never sin again." It didn't take long to find out that isn't the way it works.

However, all these years, my baptism has meant a lot to me. It was a step toward the Lord, and I've never quit taking those steps. Sometimes it's been easy, sometimes very, very hard; but Jesus has remained my friend throughout my life.

October, 1940, came and it happened AGAIN. Daddy came home from work and said, "Well, it looks like we're being transferred again. I'll know in a few days."

Was this some hateful early Halloween trick? He didn't really mean it. How could he? This was our home and we all liked it—even Mama. I would just stay in Oklahoma with my friends. Maybe Roella's mom would let me sleep at their house. Or someone!

But I never even got to ask them. Two days later Daddy came home and said he would be leaving on Sunday. He was going to the Sinclair Plant 18 in East Texas. After he found a house he would come back for us and our things.

"Texas! This is worse than I thought. I'll never move to Texas! Never!" By now, Mama was crying and talking really loud.

I kept quiet about my plans to stay with Roella. In fact, Daddy sent June and me outside to play. We sat on the porch and though we couldn't hear everything, we knew things were pretty hot inside.

Finally, he came outside and told us we could go with him to get some hamburgers for supper. I wondered why Mama wasn't getting supper for us herself.

When we got home, Mama's face was red, but she wasn't crying and she was very quiet the rest of the evening.

The morning Daddy left, all of us cried—even Daddy. "I'll see you as soon as I can." He gave each of us a hug and headed down the road with a big cloud of red dust trailing behind.

I watched till the car went over the second hill and dipped out of sight. When I turned around, Mama was standing there holding June. "Mama, what are we going to do?" I sobbed.

"Well, I think maybe we'll all sleep together in my bed tonight. Would you girls like to do that?" She started for the house talking to herself. "I don't know how it can happen, but maybe your Dad's right for once, maybe somehow it will be OK."

PART FOUR

To Texas And Back

After Daddy left, every single morning was the same. A nagging thought tugged me awake, "Maybe he came back in the night. I'll just run to the window and see if our green car is there." But there was no need to check. I knew he was still way down there in that hateful old Texas and I confided to my diary that I missed him "awfully much."

Mama took over. "We've got to settle in and get busy if we're gonna be ready when your dad comes for us." Every morning I caught the school bus. Neighbors stopped by to visit with Mama and help her pack. Sometimes they brought "a little somethin' to eat." Other times they said, "Stop over for supper with us tonight—nothin' fancy."

June was pretty confused with what was happening; she hung on to her doll and yelled, "Where Daddy?" Seems like she "acted out" a little more than usual, which meant she got more whippin's than usual.

The kids at school kept asking, "When are you leaving? I thought your daddy was coming back to get y'all."

"Well, he is, as soon as he can. He'll come, you'll see."

"Yeah? Well, when will that be?" I don't think they were being mean. They just wondered about Daddy being gone.

It was not unusual for lease families to move in and out of the community. I gave up on asking if I could stay behind with some one; I decided that even Texas would be better than Cherry Hill without Daddy.

Finally, one afternoon Mama met the school bus waving a letter. "Your dad will be here by Thanksgiving. That's next week," she smiled, "so we've got to quit foolin' around and get this packing done."

"Oh boy! Oh gosh, oh, boy! Is this really true? Hey, June, Daddy's comin' to get us. How 'bout that?" I didn't wait for an answer. I had to get my stuff together.

There were only a few days left. But my smile faded a little more as each one of those days passed, especially at school. My hiding place was long gone as the leaves had fallen, but I climbed my persimmon tree one last time. Many thoughts chased around in my mind. It wasn't that I wasn't ready to leave (I was, besides I didn't have a choice), but this place had been my real home.

The empty school building across the road caught my eye, and I thought of all the parties and programs we'd had there. I remembered all the games we'd played in that old Cherry Hill school yard, and how many times I'd been knocked down flat playing Red Rover. I understood that being knocked down was part of the game and I always got up to play again.

I wondered if there would be a Mrs. Elliott in Texas who would bring popcorn balls at Christmas time, and what about my guitar lessons? Would anyone want to listen to June and me sing our songs? As the tears began to wash down the mountain of memories I was piling up, I knew it was time to climb down. I still had things to do and maybe there would be a tree in Texas just waiting for me to climb where I could look at new memories.

With parties, and goodbyes, and promises to write, Wednesday night finally came. There was Daddy walking through the door. He was laughing and giving us all hugs and talking a mile a minute. I couldn't believe it. Gone all this time and he hadn't changed a bit!

Over the next few days, Mama and Daddy loaded our things that were going to Texas onto the long trailer parked in the driveway. It belonged to

Daddy's new Texas friends, the Swearingens. They were visiting relatives in Durant and Sunday morning they would come to get us and the trailer. We would head out for Texas together.

What a trip that was! It was crowded with eight people squeezed into one car, but Daddy and Mr. Swearingen both assured everyone, "Don't worry. We'll make Gladewater by suppertime.

And I'm sure we would have, except for a couple of problems getting in the way. Just after we stopped to eat the sandwiches Mama had made for dinner, the car started making a strange coughing sound. Before long, the motor stopped completely. Daddy and Mr. Swearingen looked under the hood. I heard the word "carburetor." Daddy usually worked on our car when something was wrong, so I thought, "He'll have it fixed in no time." I saw him shaking his head. With a frown on his face, I heard him say. "It's not far to the next town, but you know, today is Sunday. We'll see what we can find."

They walked around the car and unhitched the trailer. Then they began working under the hood again. At last the motor coughed, then started. As we pulled away, I looked out the back window; all our stuff disappeared from sight.

The car sputtered all the way to the next town. Luckily, there was an open filling station and the guy said he would take a look at the car. But, as he put it, "I can't make any guarantees on how long it will take."

"Looks like we don't have a choice," Mr. Swearingen decided. "Let's see if there's a place where Anne and Thelma can take the kids to wait."

"There's a little park right down the street if they want to wait there," suggested the filling station guy.

It was a warm day for November, so we walked to the park and waited and waited, and then waited some more. How long can four kids play in two swings and one sand pile before some serious fussing begins? After what seemed like hours, somebody yelled, "Here they come!" All but the Swearingen baby cheered.

Mr. Swearingen leaned his head out the window and said, "Looks like she's runnin' again. We're going out to pick up the trailer. Y'all go on down to that little café we passed coming into town. Go ahead and feed the kids and yourselves, and get some sandwiches and coffee for us. We'll be on our way as soon as we get back."

Daddy joined in, "Don't worry. We'll be a little later than we thought, but it's gonna be OK."

By the time we were on the road again, the sun had dropped into a hazy western horizon. The car seemed to be running OK. Everyone relaxed a little and when we crossed Red River into Texas, we were rolling right along. The "little" kids were sleeping in the quiet darkness, when Mama's screaming woke up everybody.

"Stop this car! Stop it now!"

The car was swaying from side to side and a blinding light was coming in the back window. When I turned around, there was a big fireball chasing us. By now, the kids were crying, both Mamas were yelling, Mr. Swearingen was fighting the steering wheel to get the car straightened out, and Daddy was giving encouragement, "Hang on, Fred."

"Look at that," I hollered. "There goes a wheel." I watched the runaway wheel race along beside us for a ways, then roll right on past us and down the highway until it bounced into a bar ditch and disappeared.

The car finally came to a stop on the side of the road, and just like that, the fireball went out. "Well, Fred," Daddy barked. "I guess we'd better see what the hell has happened now." As they started to get out, Mrs. Swearingen cautioned, "Watch your language. Remember the children."

Daddy made a "Humph" sound and they went to the back of the car. Seems a wheel had come off the trailer and the axle had been scraping the pavement. This had been our "fireball." I could see them standing there, shaking their heads and talking about what to do. (It seemed pretty simple to me—what they needed to do was find the wheel and put it back on the trailer.)

They must have had the same idea. I saw them walking down the road, and soon they came back rolling the wheel in front of them. I guess they had trouble getting the wheel on because a lot of time passed, and a lot of action was going on back there. The talk didn't sound "happy."

When they got back into the car, they slammed the doors and with few words, we were on our way again. No one mentioned when we might reach Gladewater.

Mama was holding June, and the rest of us kids shared the back seat with them. I thought, "Who could sleep this way," but the next thing I knew, Daddy was shaking me, "Wake up, Toots." I opened my eyes to see we were parked in front of a house set in a piney woods.

"It's too late to do anything now. We'll throw down some pallets and y'all just stay here the rest of the night." In record time, we were all in bed. I figured, "I'll never go to sleep," but before I knew it, Mama was calling me. "Come have some breakfast, and then we're going over to our new house."

After breakfast, Mr. Swearingen took us a couple of miles, across a railroad track and down to the end of a sandy lane. "This must be it. Yep! There's our green car parked out front."

I was disappointed—a three-room boomshack (unpainted as usual) and "Oh, not again!" We were back to a path that led to the outside privy.

Mr. S. helped Daddy unhitch the trailer, and after Daddy thanked him for all the help, he left.

"Here we are," said Daddy, "It's the best I could do, Thelm', so let's go on in and have a look around."

June and I followed them across the porch and into the front room. A bedroom went in one direction and the kitchen in another, not the usual shotgun house arrangement. Of course, I would sleep on the couch in the front room. "Uh, oh, wait a minute." I realized they didn't bring June's bed. "Mama, where's June gonna sleep? She doesn't have a bed. I guess she'll sleep with you and Daddy, huh?"

"Of course not, don't be silly." said Mama. "She'll sleep on the couch with you."

"Oh no! Not with me." No one had slept with me since the Grandma Corie winter. "I'll just sleep on the floor."

But as usual, I had no say in the matter, and beginning that very night the on-going fight over who was on whose side of the bed began. Actually, it continued until I left for East Central State College. June was a "cuddler" and I did not want to be touched. That was a BIG problem. I drew lines down the center, I put pillows between us, and tried anything else I could think of. I gave up "telling on her for touching me" because the answer always came back, "She's here to stay." Sometimes I wonder if any two siblings ever successfully slept in the same bed.

Although we were still living on a Sinclair lease, this one was different from the Oklahoma leases. The sky-reaching pine trees of East Texas were everywhere. The sweet gum tree in our yard was just right for climbing, and soon took the place of my persimmon tree. I guess the biggest difference was that our house was never in darkness. Just beyond the end of the road an iron pipe stretched up far above the pine trees. It burned off excess gas from the plant, and it never went out. I'd seen them at the other plants, but never this big.

Actually, we were supposed to stay away from the torch area, but there was no fence or any kind of barrier. Before long, I was joining the other camp kids in the "hot sand" contest which took place beneath the torch in the sandy area where nothing grew. We ran around barefooted on the hard sand and the last person who gave in to the burning feet was declared "winner."

Just like all other camps, this one had kids of all ages. That first evening in the camp, Max said, "The school bus doesn't cross the railroad tracks to pick us up. We all walk up there and wait together. Anyone who is late is left behind." That bus driver didn't sound too friendly.

Plant 18 was just beyond two rows of small boomshacks and a row of company houses. We'd never lived this close to the plant and Daddy almost always walked to work. This meant Mama could have the car at home. She and June could take off for Gladewater or even Longview. Mama said, "I need to know where I can find the stores with the best bargains."

The second morning we were in Texas, Mama said, "Get ready, Mildred. We've got to get you into school." From the camp, it was about five miles to White Oak, the large consolidated school that served all the surrounding gasoline camps and the small town of White Oak. "Gosh, Mama, this is the biggest school I've ever seen."

"We'll find our way," replied Mama as she parked the car in the visitors' lot.

Mama took June by the hand and we went in. She found the principal's office where she introduced herself and me. And so it was that Mama's battle with the Texas State Department of Education in general and the Principal of White Oak School in particular began.

Mama explained that we had just moved from Oklahoma, and that I was in the sixth grade. She reached into her purse for my records. The conversation went something like this.

"Now, Mz. Murphy," said Mr. Principal, "we are so glad to have your little girl with us, but you must understand that she will be placed in the fifth grade here in Texas."

"No, you misunderstood, she's in the sixth grade."

"Well, of course, but that was in Oklahoma. Texas schools are ahead of other states, so we always put out-of-state children back a year. It's nothing against your little girl, but here in Texas, we need only eleven grades of learning to graduate our students." (I was getting pretty tired of this "little girl" stuff he kept talking about.)

Mama's face was getting red. I was worried. "You know, I don't care how many grades of learning your Texas students need to graduate. This girl is not going into the fifth grade. I never heard of such a thing. She will be in the sixth grade and that's the end of it. I don't even know how long we'll be in Texas, not long I hope."

"Mz. Murphy, don't get excited. Just calm down. We have no choice in the matter!"

"You do have a choice and this is it. Here's what you're going to do. You are going to put her in the sixth grade. If she can't do the work, then maybe we'll talk about putting her back."

"We've never done that before. It's just not our way here in Texas."

"Look, Mr. Principal, Texas is not the only place in the world. I've lived in Oklahoma and I've lived in Illinois and Indiana, and their school systems are just fine. Now we're wasting time. She should be in class, not sitting around in this office."

"Illinois, you say? And Indiana? A Bluebelly! I might have known."

Oh, boy! Now he'd done it! Sparks were shooting out from Mama's eyes like it was the Fourth of July. I expected to hear a few of Aunt Lizzie's "hell-fire" words any minute. Instead, for once, Mama took a firm grip on herself. "Either get her into a sixth grade room right now, or you and your Texas schools are in for more trouble than you ever thought possible from this Bluebelly."

I ducked my head and wished I could disappear, all the while thinking, "Now Mama's really done it. I probably won't have <u>any</u> place to go to school. Besides, what if I start crying?"

Mama and the Principal went on a little longer, but he finally stood up, looked at Mama and said, "Have it your way, Mz. Murphy. When your daughter fails, just remember that this was your choice."

He turned to where I was scrunched down in the chair. "Come with me," he frowned. He started out the door and I knew he expected me to follow. I looked at Mama, who said, "Go ahead. You'll be fine. Remember your bus number is 6. I'll see you this afternoon." She grabbed June's hand and marched out. If she'd had an American flag, I'm sure she would have been waving it.

"This will be your homeroom," said the Principal. He gave my name to the teacher and left. "This isn't going very well," I thought, but I was wrong.

The teacher smiled, introduced me to the other kids and showed me where to sit. "We've just started class, so here's a book for now. I'll get the rest of your books later."

I melted into my seat and my Texas education began.

Although Mama's regard for Texas schools is better left unsaid, it didn't take long for me to feel right at home. Reading, writing, and arithmetic—I couldn't see much difference in the classes, except we had a period for Texas history where I learned a lot about the Alamo. We also had a class called Physical Education, but it was just a time when we played games. I'm sure Oklahoma called it "recess." I stayed in sixth grade with no mention of going back to fifth. Even at school, there was the same kind of kinship between the lease kids that I'd found in other places.

That spring, Eli brought his mule to plant the field next to our house. I thought "How different from the Illinois' farms," as I watched him walk down the long rows and drop the seeds from a bag. Later when he came to plow the field, his son, Eugene, came with him. Eugene and June sat in the sand at the edge of the field and played with a bucket, an old sifter and a couple of pans that Mama gave them. June chattered away while Eugene seriously sifted sand. I sat nearby under the sweet gum tree and read my books.

It was a good time for everyone, till those "ladies" came by. They brought problems! Eugene wore overalls like his dad, only they were bigger. People called Eugene retarded. But the biggest problem seemed to be that Eugene and his dad were black.

One day as I sat under the tree while June and Eugene were sifting the sand for pies, the two ladies parked in front of our house. I didn't recognize either one of them, but Mama met them at the front door and asked them to come in. I saw them shake their heads and they stayed on the porch. Mama stepped outside, and soon I could hear their angry voices getting louder.

The ladies were waving their arms around and pointing toward Eli plowing the field, and June and Eugene playing in the sand. Mama seemed to be getting upset, and I saw her point toward their car. They turned and hurried to their car, banged both doors and drove off.

I ran over to where Mama was still standing on the porch, watching the car disappear across the train tracks. "Who were those ladies, Mama? What did they want?"

She didn't really answer my questions—just shook her head, gritted her teeth and muttered something about, "I knew we should never have moved to this place." She opened the screen door, but before going in she turned to say, "They weren't 'ladies'. Now go get your sister for dinner." Mama BANGED the screen door as she went in.

The thing was that it wasn't dinner time, and when I pulled her up from her sand pies, June squalled all the way to the house and tried to bite my fingers as I dragged her along.. Eugene watched us go, then he pulled himself up and walked over to where his daddy was unhitching the mule.

After that day, Eli still came to plow the field; Eugene never came back with him. June asked Mama over and over, "Don't Eugene like me anymore? Why don't he come play with me?"

Mama just shook her head and looked at me, "Go play with your sister." Well, I had better things to do than sift sand, but I also knew better than to say so.

I think maybe now I know why Eugene never came back to play, or why his Daddy didn't wave at us any more when he came to plow, or let us pet the mule. But, still I wonder, "Would it be any different today?"

We never settled into a permanent church home in Texas. The country was so beautiful with its giant trees, rolling rivers and bubbling streams, fields of flowers and lakes covered with lily pads. Sunday would often find us "on the road." Daddy always said, "God's worked hard on creation, so we'd better appreciate it." Sometimes we would just enjoy the beauty of the drive; other times we would come upon a little country church by the roadside, and he'd say, "This looks like a good place to stop. Let's join them."

Each church was a little different, but the music was familiar and we would join right in. It was special if they were having "dinner on the ground," and invited us to join them. Sometimes we did. Even Mama had to admit, "I reckon Texas does have some good cooks."

One Saturday night Daddy made one of his announcements, "Better get to bed. We're gonna' hit the road early in the morning. Toots, you'll want to bring your guitar." Mama laid out our Sunday clothes.

The next morning Mama urged, "Eat your oatmeal (ugh!), then hurry and get dressed. Your Dad is already waiting for us."

"Where are we going, Daddy?" June joined in, "Goin' where, where?"

"You'll see," laughed Daddy. "Just enjoy the ride."

As we drove through Kilgore, I could see why it was called the oil rig town. The rigs were everywhere. People talked about the beauty of the town at Christmas when lights were strung from rig to rig. They came from all over East Texas and western Louisiana to see the beautiful sight.

Several miles south of Kilgore, we followed a sandy road till we came to a wooden school building sitting in the pines. Cars were parked everywhere. "Guess we made it," said Daddy. "Bring your guitar and let's get inside."

We could hear "Gimme that old time religion, gimme that old time religion," coming through the open windows. Seems they were having an all-day gospel sing and foot washing, with a little preaching in between.

There were only a few empty chairs on the gym floor. The stage was crowded with people holding instruments of all kinds—guitars, fiddles, mandolins, and banjos. A piano sat on each side of the stage. As I looked around, I saw that many people in the audience had musical instruments. The sound of jingling tambourines kept time with the music.

"Come on in," invited a lady wearing a long, full skirt. "There are a few seats closer to the front." She noticed my guitar and smiled, "Ah, you must play! Here we all feel free to join in at any time, either with the singing or the playing."

We found seats and soon, we joined in with the singing. Most of the songs were familiar, and Daddy leaned over and said, "Toots, you can chord these songs. Why don't you get started."

At first I wasn't sure I wanted to but, with his urging; I was chording away and having a good time. Lots of hand-clapping and "Amens" punctuated the singing.

I'd never seen anything like this. Along with the group singing, there were solos, duets, trios and quartets. They made room for anyone who wanted to go share in the music. I thought, "This must be what music from heaven sounds like. I wish I could sing and play like this." They were having such a good time.

After about an hour of singing, everyone grew quiet as a man walked to the front of the stage. I guess he was a preacher 'cause he opened the Bible and read a story about Jesus washing the feet of His disciples. I'd never heard this story before and it seemed a little strange to me. I didn't really understand why Jesus would do this thing. Shouldn't the disciples be washing Jesus' feet?

The man announced, "Let us follow our Lord's example. The foot-washing service will begin immediately in the hallway and on the porch. Singing will continue here in the gym."

Some people sitting next to Mama said, "Why don't you come out with us?" When we got outside, the people sitting on the benches were taking off their shoes. Other people held cloths and washpans. They seemed to take turns sitting on the benches or serving as foot washers. While Mama and June and I stood nearby, Daddy joined the group. We watched as a stranger washed Daddy's feet, then they changed places. Afterwards Daddy shook the man's hand.

On the way home, I asked Daddy about the foot washing. He said this was a way for people to remember Jesus and His life. "But Daddy," I wanted to know, "how does washing somebody's dirty feet help us remember Jesus?"

"Well, it's not just washing someone's dirty feet, Toots. Jesus washed the disciple's feet to show them His humility. That means you don't think you're too good to do things for other people. You help them when you can. Do you see?"

"I guess so, but I'll have to think about it."

Springtime in East Texas usually meant warm sunny days, but the nights were a different story. Around bedtime, a soft rain would start hitting the roof, and join the old familiar chug-chug of the plant engines. Come morning, I would wake up to a world of diamond raindrops sending rainbows in all directions as they were touched by the rising sun. By the time we began the walk to the bus stop, the sand was already dry.

One night was different. A few weeks earlier, Mama had pestered Daddy until he agreed to repaper the whole house—all three rooms. When they finished, Mama was peacock proud, and wrote letters to all our kinfolks describing how pretty it looked.

Then disaster struck. Just before bedtime it started raining—not the usual, soft drops; these hit the roof like a hammer. As we listened, the sounds grew louder. Daddy went to the window. "Come look at this. The hail is bigger than marbles. It's ankle deep out there."

Before long, bulges started appearing in the ceiling. "Look at that!" Mama cried. "The roof is leaking. What are we going to do now?"

Daddy assured her. "We'll take care of it. Get a knife and we'll make a little slit and let the water drain out." That worked fine for awhile, but the hail kept on falling for more than two hours. By the light of the torch, we could see the hail piling up in the yard. Like some prehistoric swamp, curls of steam were coming up from the hard sand beneath the flames. I thought of the Sinclair dinosaur and wondered if he might come lumbering along.

Before the storm passed, 37 buckets were scattered throughout the house. Mama's new wallpaper was falling off the ceilings and the walls. The water falling inside the house was matched only by Mama's tears and icy comments about "this awful, awful place." Her exact words were, "Lucian, you brought me to hell!"

June and I turned the whole thing into a game. We ran from room to room looking for the bulges, then yelling, "Bring the bucket." We would jump out of the way and cheer as a new waterfall came pouring down. Daddy tried to tell Mama, "It's gonna be OK," but there was no consoling her. She told him to, "Shut up!" He did!

In the aftermath of the "Hail Storm of '40", new tin roofs appeared on most of the houses. I wondered what kind of music that would make if we had another storm.

No matter where we lived, we went to the picture show a lot. One I'll always remember is the premier of "Gone With The Wind." The grand occasion was held in the Princess Theater in Longview. Before we even reached the theater, we could see the path of flood lights sweeping across the night sky.

I knew this would be a magic evening. Aunt Stella had sent the book at Christmas, and I read it several times before the premier. It's my all-time favorite movie and at eleven years of age, I considered Scarlett a heroine for the ages. I still find her philosophy of "I'll handle it tomorrow" very useful for some days.

Summer came and the garden was ready for canning. I helped Mama with the picking and preparing, but it seemed to me that she was resting a lot. Mama never took a nap in the day time. One day she just fell over on the floor. When I ran to her she was all white, and seemed to be asleep.

"Mama, mama, what's the matter?" I shouted. "Please wake up!" I shook her but she didn't open her eyes. Daddy was at work, and I ran across the road to get help from Mrs. Hollingsworth.

She sent her son, Max, to the plant to get Daddy. By the time he got home, Mama was awake, but she was still sitting on the floor leaning on Mrs. Hollingworth.

Daddy got her into the car to go to Gladewater to the hospital. Mrs. Hollingsworth said she would take June and me home with her, but Daddy said "No, I want them to go with me." I remember that we played with the magnolia petals under two big trees while Daddy took Mama inside the hospital.

After a long time, he came out and sat down with us. "Your mama is going to stay here at the hospital for a while. She's gonna be OK., but we're gonna see if Grandma Pearce can come down from Illinois and stay with us for awhile."

This sounded pretty scary to me. Mama never was sick. (She had a bleeding ulcer and was in the hospital for about ten days.)

When we met Grandma Pearce at the bus station, we were glad to see her. She seemed really worried and I heard her telling Daddy, "It's no wonder Thelma got sick, with all she's been through here. You know she doesn't like it." Daddy didn't say anything.

Grandma stayed for a few weeks after Mama came home, but gradually, as Mama got stronger and began doing things again, she began to talk about going home. It was the middle of July, and school would be starting soon. Grandma was still a teacher in a one-room Illinois country school.

About a month after Grandma left, Daddy came home from the plant with some news. He wasn't whistling as he usually was when he came in the door. He seemed very serious. Mama took one look at him and asked, "What's the matter?"

"Well, Thelm' it looks like we're going to be moving again. Sinclair is making some changes and a new oil field has just opened up in Casper, Wyoming."

He might as well have said, "It's on the moon." Mama jumped about that high when she heard the word "Wyoming." Before she had time to say much more than, "Listen to me! You are crazy if you think for one minute that I'm going to Wyoming," Daddy sent June and me outside to play.

While they went at each other inside, I tried to think what it would be like to move again. It wasn't like we had been in Texas that long, only nine months. I hadn't even gone to the White Oak school a whole year yet, I didn't know that many people. But what about my friends on the lease? They were good friends. And where would we go if Mama really wouldn't go to Wyoming, and what would Daddy do? How could we live if Daddy didn't have a job? "Aw, for gosh darn sakes!" I knew "darn" was a hell-fire word, but it seemed to me this was just too much!

Eventually all the questions were answered. Mama won the battle. Daddy didn't say much, but he agreed to quit his job with Sinclair. We would go to Illinois and stay at Grandma's house till something could be decided.

The few things they didn't sell, Mama and Daddy packed into a small trailer hitched to the green car. My friends had a little party and gave me a box of stationery. We promised to write letters, and we did for awhile.

Less than a week later, we pulled out early one morning just as the sun topped the piney woods. As we bumped across the train tracks, I looked back at the torch and our house where it was never really night. I could see Eli's field where the corn was about ready for harvest, and my sweet gum haven for reading. With a sigh, I turned my face to the North.

Four days later we pulled into Grandma's yard in Marshall, Illinois. It was time to begin again. Daddy said it would be OK, but right then, his promise seemed to be more of a question than a sure thing.

Grandma had supper ready when we got there, and we were ready for it. During the meal, the grown-ups talked about the trip up from Texas and family stuff. June tried to interrupt with her chatter but Mama shushed her. I ate my supper without a word. Finally, they got around to the plan for living at Grandma's.

Grandma seemed to have it all worked out. "School will start for Martha and me in a couple of weeks. Thelma, you can keep the house and take care of June and Tommy during the day. (Aunt Martha was taking care of Aunt Stella's eight-month old son, Tommy, until she and Uncle Bob could take him to Chicago to live.) Of course, Mildred must be enrolled in Northside Elementary and Lucian you will be looking for work. I asked around and Milo told me the railroad is hiring section hands for the rest of the season. With this big, two-story house, there should be plenty of room for all of us."

Nobody said much—not even Daddy. When Grandma took over, it usually happened just that way!

Illinois farmers are partial to August. It's a hot, humid time. They say things like, "This is good weather for the crops." and "My corn grew three inches overnight." But, there was no corn growing in that upstairs bedroom where I slept. Even with the windows open, no wind came in at night. (I missed the Oklahoma wind that cooled things off in the evenings.) That pest, "snuggling June" was still my bed partner, and sometimes, at night I would take my pillow downstairs and sleep on the floor.

The first couple of weeks we were at Grandma's, it seemed like we were on vacation. We went to the Clark County Fair every night. Even though it made me a little sick at my stomach, I rode on the ferris-wheel and the merry-go-round. I always won a prize at the "guess-your-age" booth, because the guy would guess me younger than I really was.

Cotton candy was my favorite treat and I became be a sticky, gooey mess by the time the horse sulky races were over. The cousins and I had a great time.

After fair week, I stayed with the farm cousins. It was while I was there that I realized how much I missed the open spaces of the lease. I'd never lived in a town—not even a small one like Marshall. I wasn't sure I liked it much. I hoped when we found a new place to live, it would be in the country.

Beginning the third week, we settled into something resembling the routine Grandma had laid out that first night. Daddy did find temporary work as a section hand repairing the railroad tracks. He said it would last until cold weather came. Mama kept the house, took care of Tommy, who rattled his play pen and seemed to cry a lot. June had already found a new sand pile and a friend who helped her make pies.

On Monday, Mama took me to Northside Elementary where I joined the seventh graders. (No hassels this time about what grade I should enter.) The school was about six blocks from Grandma's house. Walking to school was like taking a stroll through an autumn art gallery. The trees on each side of eighth street came together in an arch of brilliant fall colors which changed every day. No sooner would I start my walk when, one by one, other kids would join in. By the time we reached school, there would be nearly a dozen of us. It was a quick, easy way to make friends.

My favorite subject was Mrs. Bennett's English class. Every other week she had a story day, much like the one we'd had at Saint Louis. Each person wrote a story, then read it to the class. It was a time for my imagination to swirl like snow flakes in the wind. What fun!

Once a month we had "talent day." Students sang, played instruments, recited poems and one kid had a magic act. I would wear my boots, take my guitar and sing a good ole western song. My classmates liked "Wabash Cannon Ball" best and as I plucked away, they would join in on the chorus. One of my kissin' cousins started calling me "Cannon Ball." Thank goodness, only a few other kids picked up on it.

The Courthouse square was the social gathering place for Marshall. Throughout the summer and early fall, on Friday nights, people brought folding chairs and blankets to sit on the grass while the Marshall Community Band gave a concert. It was a chance for the farmers to catch up on the country news—"How's the corn and beans look out your way?" to "Has Susie had the baby yet?" to "How did Marie's pickles do at the fair this year?"

Anyone who had a nickel could buy a bag of popcorn at the popcorn-wagon. The guy must have sold tons of popcorn 'cause he'd been sitting on that same corner every Friday and Saturday night since I could remember.

Groups of girls and groups of boys around my age stood around and talked, but rarely together. I don't know what the boys talked about, but they were the main topic of the girls' conversations. Just the mention of a boy's name could bring on a fit of the giggles. I pretended I knew exactly what they were talking about and giggled as much as anyone. It was about this time in my life that I began to suspect that there was a big difference between "boy" friends (I had had several) and a "boyfriend" (I had none).

Not having a boyfriend was not necessarily by choice. In fact, there was one pretty cute boy who walked to school with us. Bobby Wilson would come running out of his house, still eating breakfast most mornings. His friendly "hello" could fluster me in a big way. I tried to plan ahead so I would have something really intriguing to say. It never worked. I just smiled and said "Hi," or some dumb thing like, "Do you think it will rain today?"

Just when I thought things might be swinging my way, a friend whispered in my ear, "Don't get too interested in Bobby. He's Patty Moriarty's boyfriend. You know, she's the girl with the long blond curls."

"Oh, no! Not another girl with blond curls. Shades of Bonnie Jean! How can this be fair?"

Sometimes after school, we would walk down town to the Candy Kitchen to have a Coke. This was the local hang out for teens, but twelve-year-olds like me were not turned away. It was here that I learned to dance—well, sort of. "Elmer's Tune" was the most-played song, and the Jitterbug was the dance. At that point, I danced with boys only in my dreams, so we girls tried to teach each other. As long as I didn't trip and moved my feet around with the beat of the music, I could call it dancing.

I would sit in a booth, sipping my coke and watch the older boys and girls doing the fancy steps. "What would I say," I wondered, "if Bobby Wilson should ask me to dance?" It seemed a little hopeless that any <u>boy</u> would ever ask me. I don't think a single one in that Candy Kitchen ever did, but that didn't keep me from going and having a good time. When it was time to start home, sometimes I would slip in a little "Hubba, hubba" just to be a part of the gang.

As the days passed, it was not unusual to see boys in uniforms on the streets of Marshall. When Bud Veach (Aunt Fern's brother) came home on leave, he dropped by Grandma's house for a visit. He had just finished basic training in the Army at Ft. Leonardwood in the Ozarks. I felt very important because he sat on the front porch and talked with "just me" for a while. He talked about the Ozarks and told me how pretty they were.

Bud seemed excited about what might be ahead for him. He wondered if he would get to visit a foreign country. (When the word came later that he had been killed on the beaches of Anzio, I thought a lot about that day when we sat on Grandma's front porch and talked. I wondered if he had been able to see some things in any other country before his life ended on that beach. I wondered if his mama thought it was worth it.)

By Thanksgiving, it was getting cold in Illinois and Daddy's job with the section hands ended. He looked for another job, but they were scarce. He fixed things at Grandma's house and helped out on the farms—though harvest season was soon over.

On Thanksgiving Day we had a big Pearce family dinner with turkey and all the extras. Mama made cornbread dressing, something she had learned in Oklahoma. Aunt Stella and Uncle Bob came down from Chicago and after the holiday, Tommy went home with them. It seemed really quiet at the house after he was gone.

A few days later, Mama left about suppertime. She said she would be gone for awhile; when she came home the next morning she was smiling. "Virgie and Milo have a new baby girl." She told Grandma they named her Doris Kay.

When I went to see my new baby cousin, I remembered how June had looked that first day, all red and wrinkled, and I wondered if all new babies looked the same. I wondered, "If they were put all together in a row, could anyone tell them apart?" I guess maybe Moms could.

Grandma had a big Baby Grand piano sitting in what she called the "music room." One afternoon I was picking out a song, wondering if I could ever learn to play a piano. Daddy came in and sat on the bench beside me.

"How are things going here in Illinois?" he asked.

"OK. I guess. Sometimes I wish we still lived on the lease, but I guess we can't. It just seems like we're on vacation or something without our own house."

"I know," he said. "but we'll find a place soon." He picked out a little song on the piano before he said, "You know, Toots, you are growing up. Changes are happening and we should have a little talk about that."

I had a feeling that something else was coming that I might not like. I just looked at him and waited.

"As you get older, your body begins to change. Some of these changes are outside. You know, like you get taller or your feet get bigger; but other changes are happening inside. Do you remember the picture show we saw about the Miracle of Life?"

"Sure, the one about the new baby. I thought about it when Aunt Virgie got her new baby last month."

"That's right. And a time comes for every girl when her body begins to get ready to become a lady, because some day the lady may want to become a Mom."

My words came tumbling out. "Well, I guess, someday maybe, but not for a long, long, long time. So, Daddy, what in the world are you talking about? What are all these inside changes. Does it hurt? When will this happen? How will I know? Will anybody else know?"

So, as we sat together in the quiet of the music room, Daddy explained to me the mysteries of menstruation. He ended by saying, "It's a nature thing, it doesn't mean you're different and there is nothing to be scared about. You'll know when it happens, and Mama will give you what you need to take care of it." He gave me a little hug and that ended my "birds and bees" discussion.

I really had heard nothing about this before, and I didn't talk about it to anyone. I waited for a few days for something to happen. When it didn't, I put it aside, and it was months later before I had to think about it again.

One thing I liked about living in Illinois was that we were able to go to my grandfather's church again. That was very special. Sundays began with Sunday School and church, followed by a fried chicken dinner at one of the relative's houses, then games or singing, depending on the weather, and back to church on Sunday night. At many of the night services, I would play my guitar for group singing. Sometimes Cousin Chris and Marthell would join in with their mandolin and fiddle. It was so peaceful and it seemed Jesus often smiled on us in that country church.

One Sunday night was different. For a December day, the weather had been warm and all the kids had spent most of the afternoon playing outside. By the time we got back to church, everybody was tired. But it seemed more than that. No doubt about it! Something was going on. I noticed there wasn't much of the usual friendly chatter, no one had even mentioned the group singing. Instead, Brother Watkins stepped behind the pulpit and we quietly found our places in the pews.

Brother Watkins began. "My brother was in that little skirmish in the Pacific today?" Heads turned. "What's he talking about?" "What little skirmish?"

He said a few words, prayed, and we sang one song. The service ended. People gathered around and he answered the big question. "The Japanese bombed Pearl Harbor today."

There was a stunned silence. (Remember: no CNN and few people listened to radios on a Sunday afternoon.) Finally, my Uncle Zenas asked in unbelief, "Pastor, are you sure?"

Quietly he answered, "I'm sure! Let's have prayer together, and then we'll just go on home."

The next morning, December 8, 1941, the sun came up at Grandma's house and we didn't do anything different. Mama got breakfast, Daddy went to a temporary job he'd found, Grandma and Aunt Martha went to school and I went to Northside.

When we got there, it was so quiet; hardly anyone was in the hall. The teachers and kids were gathered in three or four rooms listening to radios. News was sent back and forth between the rooms, and before the day was over, the United States was at war with Japan. Three days later Germany and Italy declared war on the United States.

And so, it began!

The teachers had been getting ready for the Christmas play, and they tried to keep activities as normal as possible. Everyone in school and around town was talking of attacks and sabotage and all the other things that could happen. Newspapers ran pictures of boys standing in line to join the Army and Navy. It seemed to me we were awfully far from those countries they were talking about. At Northside Elementary, we had the Christmas play and our party a little early, and school closed for Christmas vacation.

Daddy said, "War or no war, we're going to have a Christmas tree." He picked out a big one and when it was all decorated he said, "It's the prettiest one ever." On Christmas Eve, all the Pearces, (aunts, uncles and cousins) came to Grandma's to have supper together and open presents. What a great time, and the big surprise just topped it off.

Aunt Martha was considered by some to be an "old-maid school teacher." She was a school teacher, she wasn't married, but she really wasn't THAT old. She and a Clarksville farmer had been going around together for a long time. He'd been invited to the party and we all wondered what he would get Aunt Martha for Christmas. I made sure I was sitting next to her when she got his present. When it was just a box of candy, she seemed a little disappointed, but said "Thank you" all proper like. As she started to set it aside, Francis (her boyfriend) said "Why don't you try a piece, Martha. I think you'll like the one wrapped in silver paper."

She didn't seem to want to, but she opened the box and reached in. As she unwrapped the silver foil, her eyes got bigger and bigger. As she closed her fingers around the candy, tears came into her eyes. When she opened her fingers, we all could see that it wasn't candy she was holding. It was an engagement ring! Everyone was surprised, including Aunt Martha.

"Congratulations," came from all over the room. I was happy 'cause I liked Francis a lot. He could tell really good stories. I don't know if Daddy was in on the joke or not, but he sure did laugh. Aunt Martha finally told him to "Shut up!"

After Christmas, I was glad to see some nice days. Daddy had promised to teach me how to ride my new bicycle. Well, it wasn't really new. I wanted a bicycle so bad, but Mama said "Santa Claus will not be able to bring one this year." By then, I'd figured out that Christmas presents didn't have a whole lot to do with Santa Claus.

When I knew that there would be no bicycle under the Christmas tree, I found a way to make some money. I could sell Christmas cards and for every box I sold, I could keep a quarter for myself.

Daddy said I could do it, so I walked up and down the streets and knocked on almost every door in town. Grandma said, "Be sure they know you're Jessie Pearce's granddaughter. I made sure they knew who <u>all</u> of my relatives were, and then I took orders. The cards came in well before Christmas and I delivered them. "Don't forget to say thank you," cautioned Mama . "You might want to sell something else sometime."

"OK," I said, but in my heart, I knew my door-to-door sales experience wasn't going far. As I collected the money, I sent part of it to the card company and hid my part in a box under my socks. By the time all deliveries were made, I had $25.50 in my box. I took it to Daddy and said, "We need to find me a bicycle."

The one we settled on was beautiful—red paint almost like new, butterfly handle bars, oversized padded seat, a light and a horn. What a bicycle!

Grandma lived on a graveled street, so Daddy thought we should go over to Sixth Street to practice. It was blacktopped and should be easier riding. Of course, Mama and June had to go along for the show,

Before we finished, I managed to keep the bike straight for a few feet without falling over. Daddy encouraged me, "Now it will just take practice."

As I started to push the bike home, Mama said, "Wait a minute, I want to learn to ride, too." This didn't sound too good to me, but Daddy said, "O.K. give me the bike. Get on Spanky."

I was afraid to look. Mama got on the bicycle, and Daddy caught hold of the back rack. He told Mama to pedal slowly and he would hold her up. She was doing OK when she started, but she soon decided she wanted to go faster. She pumped the pedals harder.

"Slow down," cautioned Daddy. He was running, trying to keep hold of the bike.

"Turn me loose. I'm doin' good. Turn me loose right now," commanded Mama as she pedaled faster.

Daddy had no choice. He turned her loose and she flew down the street, up a driveway and crashed into a bush. "I'm OK. Don't help me." She got up, brushed Daddy aside and started a fast pace for home. I rescued my bicycle and checked it for scratches before pushing it home. Daddy tried to catch up with Mama. June and I tried to keep our giggles quiet as we walked home together.

As far as I know, Mama's bicycle experiences ended there in the bushes. As for me, I treasured that beautiful red bicycle and rode it for years.

Just after New Year's Day a heavy snow began to fall. June was excited as this was her first memory of snow. Then, the unexpected happened again. Daddy got a telegram, which created quite a stir—but the news was good. The need for oil to fuel the war planes and tanks had brought back the chugging of wells pumping and new wells being drilled; workers were needed in the Oklahoma oil fields again. Mr. Elliott said a job was waiting for Daddy at the Sinclair plant in Saint Louis.

This time there was not a lot of discussion; in fact, there was none. Daddy declared, "We're going," For once, Mama was silent.

For me, that telegram meant only one thing, I was "going home!"

PART FIVE

Home Again

A midwinter January cold spell had gripped central Illinois and was reluctant to let go. The treacherous icy layer hidden beneath the fresh snow made packing the car and trailer slow going. Mama and Daddy did a lot of slipping as they carried our stuff down the steps of Grandma's porch. Mama kept warning, "Will you watch it! All we need is for you to fall and break a leg."

"Now Thelm', just take it easy." Daddy gave her a pat on the fanny. "Look at all these boxes we never unpacked from Texas. We'll be on the road before you know it."

"Yeah, yeah, I know. It's gonna be OK. Well, I don't want to hear it." It wasn't too hard to figure out that Mama wasn't real happy.

That wasn't my worry. As more and more stuff went out the door, I wondered, "Is there gonna be room for my bike?" Daddy came in to warm up, and as he shoveled more coal into the big potbelly stove, I reminded him, "Daddy, don't forget my bicycle. You know we have to take it. There's no one here to ride it."

"Well, I don't know, Toots. There's not much room left out there." I caught the twinkle in his eye as he went on. "Maybe you'd better see if you can find a place for it."

"Get your coat on," shouted Mama. Well, forget that. I pretended I didn't hear her as I ran down the steps to the back of the trailer. There it was, already tied in place. All the way to Oklahoma at every stop, I checked to make sure the bike was still there. I'd worked hard for that bike and I didn't intend to lose it.

The loading was finished and by early afternoon, the sun came out and cleared the roads. Just like always when we moved, it was hard for Mama. This time she was leaving her childhood home again. But, except for a few tears when she kissed Grandma goodbye, she said nothing. She knew Daddy was right, "Thelm', we don't have a choice; you know we've got to go."

The car window framed a picture very different from the Ozark summer scene. Black fingers of leafless trees stretched upward between the emerald green pines. Patches of snow dotted the valley fields. With the sweet fruit of August long gone, the empty grape stands stood with gaping doors—lonely eyes watching the cars pass by.

Night came on and June and I curled up in our little spaces between the boxes. My eyes grew heavy; every turn of the wheels sang the song, "Goin' home, goin' home!"

We reached Seminole the next day and drove out toward Plant 12. "We'd better let Bob and Lizzie know we're back." They were a surprised when we pulled up their drive. Bob told Daddy, "Plant 12 is running at top production and workers are being hired."

I cringed inside, "No! No! Don't listen Daddy. I don't want to live in Seminole." I started breathing again when Daddy told him we were going back to Saint Louis.

Lizzie insisted we have something to eat before we left. They told us about the big explosion that rocked Plant 12 while we were in Texas. Some man carelessly threw a cigarette into a tiny stream of gasoline coming from a leaking tank. It was a terrible accident. One man was killed, thirty tanks blew up, and several houses were burned.

"I was so scared," said Lizzie. "Every time another tank went up, I thought the end of the world had come."

Finally, Daddy said we'd better get moving. When we left Maud behind, I knew we were almost there. As we made the turn at McGuffey's General Store, everything looked pretty much the same and they sure hadn't done anything with the road. Daddy was growling before we'd gone more that a few feet, "I see Scott's 'Mile of Smiles' still has every bump and hole in place. Looks to me like our road commissioner hasn't fixed his grader yet."

Mr. Elliott had found an empty house for us and we stopped by the plant to pick up the key. He said Mrs. Elliott wanted to see us. While he and Daddy talked about work schedules, Mama and June and I walked across the road to see Mrs. Elliott. She hugged us and said, "I'm so glad to have you back. I have something for you." When we returned to the car, Mama was carrying a big Lazy Dazy cake, my favorite kind.

Daddy would start to work in two days. Under her breath Mama said, "Well, nothing's changed. How are we supposed to get settled in two days?"

The house was down the road from where we'd lived before, the usual three-room shotgun style with a path. I guess on oil leases, some things never change! There was not one tree even close to the house, and it didn't take long to discover the yard was full of sticker burrs and goatheads. Even as she unpacked, Mama was planning wallpaper and paint colors. "We'll have this place in shape in no time," she told friends who came by to welcome us home with the usual "little somethin'" for supper.

Mama told Daddy they would look for a stove and ice box and a couch/bed the next day, but that first night June and I slept on the floor (separate pallets at least). I listened carefully. Sure enough, after five months of night-time silence, the chugging lease lullaby was right in tune.

The next morning, before going shopping, Mama took time out to take me to school. The second semester of the seventh grade had just started. Everyone was surprised to see me, but the same teachers were sitting behind the desks. I knew most of the kids in the room. By lunch, it was almost as if I'd never been away.

Miss Casselman gave me a hug and said, "I'm so glad to see you. The Mother Goose operetta is just days away and our 'Miss Muffet' moved last week. You will be perfect for the part."

"I guess so." I soon found out it doesn't take a lot of talent to sit on a tuffet and pretend to eat "curds and whey." My only lines were a loud scream when the giant spider came crawling my way. Then I ran off the stage till the final curtain.

What a great way to begin my homecoming! One thing hadn't changed—the girl with the golden curls was Bo Peep and she was the "star" of the show. She used her shepherd's staff like a scepter to rule over all the other Mother Goose characters.

As the wind turned South, an early spring softened the winter chill. The winds of change blew all around us—some good, some not so good. New derricks appeared and old ones were strung with working lights for the night crews. The news from the Pacific grew worse and the need for oil increased.

Daddy's new job at the plant meant he would work shift work. The hours rotated every week—days, evenings and midnights—with Tuesday and Wednesday off. This remained his schedule for the rest of his Sinclair working time.

This meant big-time changes for our family. We'd always had five days for working, with Saturday for shopping and the picture show, and Sunday for Sunday School and church. Supper time had always been family talk time at our house.

Now everything revolved around which shift Daddy was working. Very often Mama and June and I did things without Daddy because he was working. At home, Mama was always "shushing" us because Daddy was sleeping. We soon found out that Daddy slept whether it was quiet or not; so home activities returned to something like normal, no matter what the shift.

The war dominated almost every conversation. People everywhere were talking about how, "we're gonna take these guys out and this whole thing will be over before they know it," but it didn't happen. Posters reminded us that "Loose lips sink ships!" I wondered what I could possibly know that would sink a ship.

One day it dawned on me, "This war is about so much more than me coming home." Our main news sources were the Shawnee News Star and the 6:00 evening news on the radio. A sobering reality came from the Pathfinder News on Saturday night at the Arcadia Theater. There we saw the beaches of Anzio and Iwo Jima and later, D-day names like Omaha and Utah filled with soldiers and the smoke of battles. The bombers raining destruction in England and France and Germany; the planes lifting off the Pacific aircraft carriers—all the sounds of death filled our ears. I closed my eyes and covered my ears. It was too much, and I remembered something General Sherman said as he destroyed the beauty of so much of the Southland—War is hell!

I thought about the front-page picture of that "smiling little man," who stood on the Capitol steps and talked about peace, even as the bombs fell on Pearl Harbor. I guess I "hated" the Japanese and the Germans because we were supposed to. "They" were evil and causing all this grief. Almost all of the cartoons at the picture show were about these "bad" people; but, even though they were cartoons, they didn't seem very funny to me.

Sometimes other thoughts would creep in. "Isn't Whitey Seifried a German? Didn't Mrs. Seifried help when June was born? Aren't they are our friends? I know we like them. Besides, didn't Jesus' say to love everybody?" Did He mean everybody except the "Japs" and "Germans?" It was a puzzle too hard to figure out.

Besides, I had other things on my mind. I turned thirteen that summer. No longer was I skinny as a corn stalk. The corn stalk had developed a couple of nubbins, and in one day I moved from a "cute" little girl to a gawky teenager. That "happening" that Daddy had talked about finally happened.

I went to Mama and told her "I guess I need a little help here. Do you have something for me?" She gave a big sigh and came back from her bedroom with a little sack. She handed it to me with words that would become very familiar over the next few years, "Just don't forget what I'm telling you. Don't you dare go out there and do something that will disgrace us all. This isn't going away for a long, long time."

"What in the world are you talking about, Mama? How am I gonna disgrace you?"

"Don't act like you don't know what I'm talking about. Getting in the family way is what I mean, and if that ever happened, I would never be able to hold my head up again."

"My good gosh," I thought. "I'm only thirteen years old. Why would I want to get in the family way?" I assured her I would never do anything like that, but once in awhile she would remind me all over again, especially after boyfriends came into the picture.

I soon discovered that the "happening" was more of a bother than anything else. I tried to ignore it as much as possible, but I knew if Mama was right (and she usually was), this thing wasn't going away, so I would just deal with it.

My last year in grade school was one of continual changes. For the first time I could "go out" for a place on the basketball team. I was small for a basketball player, and as Uncle Milo would say, "I wasn't worth shucks," but I loved the game and practiced hard. For the next five years, I suffered every September through the posting of the names of those who would get a suit.

Each year I was chosen, and though most of my time was spent cheering from the bench, I was a team member. It was a different game then—each team had three guards and three forwards. Players didn't cross the center line and could dribble only one time. Since I couldn't hit the basket very well, I played as a guard. My outstanding talent was that I fouled a lot and occasionally I could steal the ball.

My Senior year, I had earned a starting place on the team. "This will be a good year," I thought. But, wouldn't you know! Around Thanksgiving, my tonsils had to come out. By the time I could play again, I was back on the bench. Still, playing the game was fun, and I wore my red, satin suit with great Tiger pride.

Because of gas rationing, transportation to the games was a real problem. In grade school we depended on parents to take us. When time for the eighth grade tournament finals came, no parents showed up. Eight disappointed girls looked to Mrs. Womack for an answer. What could we do?

Mr. and Mrs. Womack (he was school superintendent, she was our coach) talked it over. They sat us down and T.L. said, "Here's what we can do. We'll take you all in our car (a '37 Ford sedan).."

"All of us? In that car? How can we fit?"

"Two of you can sit up front with Mrs. Womack and me. Four of you can fit in the back seat." We looked at each other. That left two.

"Mildred, you and Norma Ann are the smallest. You can fit in the trunk."

"In the trunk? OK, if you say so." Norma Ann and I looked at each other. We both knew no way were we gonna stay behind. What if someone fouled out? They had to have substitutes.

We watched Mr. Womack take everything out of the trunk except the spare tire. "Crawl in," he said. We did and he put some basketball suits around us. If we hunched over a little, we could just barely sit up.

"I won't close the lid all the way," he assured us. Somehow he propped it open a little. Still it was dark and as we left the school, Norma Ann and I held hands and we didn't turn loose until we reached Harjo (about 15 miles away). It was scary, but we would have done anything to go to the game.

And it was worth it. We played hard and received the second place trophy. No team <u>ever</u> beat Harjo in those days. As a reward, Mr. Womack "let us" talk him into stopping by the Saturday night preview at the Acadia in Maud.

Mama wasn't too happy with my unusual ride, but Daddy was proud of our trophy. "I wish I could have seen your game," he told me, "but you know with the way I work, I can't always go with you."

"Aw, it's O.K., Daddy. I know you can't be there everytime."

In high school, the boys and girls went to the games on the same school bus. We played on Tuesday and Friday nights, girls first, then the boys. The ride was even better if you were lucky enough to have a "player" boyfriend. And I did, part of the time.

With gasoline rationed, the school had barely enough to make the bus routes. For every game, we wondered if there would be enough to go. Mrs. Womack told me years later that on game days, a drum of "drip" gasoline would mysteriously appear at the bus garage. She said, "T. L. never questioned where it came from, or who brought it. He just filled the bus tank, loaded the players, and we were off to the game."

I think one reason I couldn't make baskets was because I couldn't see the basket. I had known for a while that I couldn't see as well as the other kids. Someone would say, "Oh look at the airplane." I would look and say, "Oh yeah," but no matter how much I squinted, I saw nothing except blue sky.

When I couldn't read the writing on the blackboard, I'd make an excuse to get really close, try to memorize what was there and then sit down. Some people thought I was a little "snooty" because I didn't always speak to them. The truth was I didn't always recognize people from a distance.

Finally the school sent a note home saying, "We believe Mildred's eyes should be tested. She seems to have some trouble seeing the board."

What a mess! There would be NO glasses! I seriously thought about "losing" the note on the way home, but knew that wouldn't work. Daddy said, "They are probably wrong," but when he asked me to read the headlines from across the room and I said, "Can you gimme' a hint?" he knew there was a problem.

Early one gloomy morning we headed for the City. Usually, I would have been excited about a trip to Oklahoma City; but this time I felt sick. I knew I wasn't gonna like this.

We climbed four flights of stairs, and entered the doctor's office. After some questions, he began the examination. I didn't like the little "tsk, tsk" sounds he made as he looked into my eyes. I could barely see the chart with shadowy black shapes. I knew they were letters, but I couldn't fake reading them.

At last, he handed me a pair of glasses and said, "I want you to take these down to the sidewalk, put them on and look around. Then come back and tell us what you think."

When I reached the street, I put on the glasses. What a shock! Even through the rain, I could read signs in the next block. People's faces were sharp. There was no softness to anything, no fuzzy edges—just a harshness that I didn't like. Those weren't raindrops running down my cheeks..

I jerked off the glasses, stomped up the stairs and back into the office. "What was it like?" asked Mama as I came through the door. Daddy joined in, "Toots, could you see everything?" The Doctor was smiling as if he'd just created the world.

I had wiped away the tears and raindrops. I sure wasn't gonna let them know how I really felt. I begged Daddy, "Do I really have to wear these? I don't think they fit."

The doctor stepped over and took the practice pair. "You'll get used to your own glasses and you'll never want to be without them. They will come in the mail in a few days." He patted my shoulder, but I pulled away. I hated the whole idea, and decided it was all his fault.

When the package came a few days later, I tore it open. The ugly things were in a little case. I ran to the mirror and put them on. I could see my round face and my straight brown hair better than I wanted to. I had covered up the only pretty part about me—my big brown eyes. The picture in the mirror was of the "not pretty girl who just got not prettier."

"Ooh, e-e! You look funny!" But who cared what goofy June thought?

"Just shut up!" I ran outside with the dumb things. There was no tree where I could hide. I walked down to the creek and sat on the bank. As I watched the red water trickling along, I wished I could just throw the glasses in and let them float away. I said, "I'm not gonna cry about this." But I did.

I considered severe myopia to be a curse from the wicked witch of the west, and for the next several years, I became an expert at faking seeing. I wore my glasses in my pocket much more than on my face.

When driving time came, I had no choice. If I was going to drive, it had to be with the glasses on. That was my only concession to wearing them. It took a very long time before I discovered "who I was" had nothing to do with a pair of glasses sitting on my nose.

In 1942, June started first grade. I had just become a teenager. Because she wasn't in my building, she wasn't a problem for me at school, but she was an embarrassment waiting to happen on the school bus. All classes started at nine o'clock and all ages rode the same bus.

June must have been allergic to everything God ever created. She had severe hay fever year round. Mama put pockets on all of her dresses with handkerchiefs in each pocket. When she sneezed, June needed these handkerchiefs in the worst way; but she very often lost them before she got out the door at home.

I made it a point to go to the back of the bus to sit with a friend. June knew she was to sit at the front of the bus, as far away from me as possible. But at least three times a week, the unthinkable happened. I would hear this loud series of sneezes, followed by a cry, "Noy, Noy, (her name for me) I can't find my hankie." I couldn't ignore this; I wanted to, but I couldn't. She was such a tattletale.

She would be standing in the middle of the aisle, with snot running down her face, off her chin, and onto her dress, still screaming, "Noy, Noy, You know Mama said you got to help me."

All I could do was pull out one of the extra hankies Mama had given me, stomp down the aisle and begin the mop up. After I finished and put another hankie in her pocket, I would sit her down with instructions, "Now, June, you sit down and stay there. If you sneeze again, you get out this hankie and don't you dare call me again." Then I would stomp back to my seat. After awhile, the kids didn't even laugh at us.

One evening I came home from school and Mama met me at the door. "You can't come in." There was a sign tacked on the house—QUARANTINE Stay away!

"What do you mean, I can't come in?"

Mama explained, "Your Daddy and I took your sister to Seminole to the doctor today. She has scarlet fever, so we are quarantined. Your Dad can go to work and come home. That's it!"

I couldn't believe all this. I knew June had been sick, but she was sick a lot.

Mama went on, "You can't stay here. We've taken your clothes up to Ingram's and you'll have to stay with them for about three weeks."

"But, Mama, I don't want to stay with them. I want to stay here or with some of my friends. Where's June? I want to see her."

"She's asleep. I told you, Mildred, you cannot come in. We can't have you sick too; besides, you need to go to school. Your daddy will be home from work in a little bit and he can talk to you. Wait for him here on the porch."

Mama went back inside and I sat down and waited. When Daddy came, he sat down with me. "This won't be so bad," he said. "You can come down and visit through the window. Ingram's said they would like having you stay there."

"But, Daddy, I want to see June. Where did she get this "scarlet fever" anyway? Is she gonna be OK?"

"Well, of course she is. Everything's gonna be OK. The time will go by before you know it. We'd better go now." I didn't want to but I got into the car. Ingram's lived less than a mile away, but when I waved goodbye as he backed out of their driveway, it seemed to me that I might as well have been left at the North Pole.

It was a long three weeks. Sometimes I would walk down home and talk to Mama and Daddy and June through the window. Different friends dropped off groceries on their front porch. Some of the kids at schools said, "Don't get too close to Mildred. You might get the scarlet fever." The only other person to have it that I know of was Roella's brother, Lindell. She was quarantined with her family and didn't even get to go to school.

Finally, after what seemed like forever, I went down for my "through the window" visit. I couldn't believe it, the sign was gone. I thought maybe it blew away, but Mama said a county person had come and taken it down. The QUARANTINE was over. Mama said, "Just one more day and you can come home." I was so happy I didn't ask why I had to wait another day.

The next night, I didn't even make a fuss about June getting too close to me. The Ingrams had been nice, but it was really good to be home.

In the fall, when Mama said we were going to move, I was fit to be tied. Not again! I thought we were here to stay. But we weren't leaving Cherry Hill. In fact, we were moving only about a hundred yards up the road. When I heard that, I knew it was good news.

It was a bigger house painted white and it had a <u>bathroom</u>. The best part was that instead of sleeping in the living room, June and I would have our very own room. For the first time ever, we would have a bed, still to be shared, but a bed instead of a couch. It was a big room with lots of windows and Mama said we could fix it up any way we wanted to.

We had our own dressing table with a mirror, chairs and drawers to put stuff in. June had her own toy box, and I had a place for my treasures. It was the best house we had ever lived in.

Outside was a wash house, a garage, and another building. Daddy decided the building was just right for raising rabbits. Because of the war, beef was rationed and other meats were scarce.

Rabbits weren't a new thing for us. When I was a little girl, before we moved to Oklahoma, I remember rows and rows of white rabbits in the big barn behind our house on the truck farm.

I helped Daddy build eight or ten cages, and before long each one was home to a rabbit. June and I liked to pet these gentle soft, white animals. "That's not a good idea," said Daddy. "You know we are raising these to sell. It's a part of the war effort." I tried not to think about the frying pan destination.

It was my job to feed the rabbits. One afternoon when I took in the bucket of feed, one of the rabbits seemed a little agitated and kept jumping in and out of her box. "What's the matter with you?" To my surprise, the next time she jumped, she left a tiny pink baby on the wire cage floor. "Oh my gosh, she must be having baby bunnies."

Since Daddy was on the day shift, I ran in to tell Mama. She said, "Your dad will take care of it when he comes home."

"But Mama, the baby is on the wire. It might die if we don't do something."

"I said your dad will take care of it. Now go finish feeding the other rabbits and leave that one alone." Mama didn't much care for the rabbits.

When I went back into the building, the Mama Rabbit was in her box again and she didn't come out. The baby was gone. Later that evening when Daddy checked on things, he said there were six babies in the nesting box.

"Do you think the Mama took the baby into the box?" I asked Daddy. "I don't know," he said. "She may have. You never can tell what happened to it."

I hoped the Mama did take care of the baby. I didn't want to think that I didn't help it.

We kept the rabbit pellets in a big barrel in the garage. Once when I went to fill my bucket from the barrel, I noticed the cover was moved a little. When I took it off, I nearly fell over when I looked inside. There wasn't much feed left, and in the bottom of the barrel was a large rat. His crazed eyes held mine. It was no secret that I didn't like mice; rats were worse.

I had to do something. But what? I decided I would hit the rat in the head and kill it, or at least knock it out. I picked up a heavy wire brush off the work bench and went back to the barrel. The rat was still on the bottom with beady eyes blazing. Slowly, slowly, I started moving the wire brush down into the barrel. I was ready to smash that rat. I didn't want to miss his wicked head.

When my hand was about half way down, the rat made his move. With teeth bared, he jumped and slashed the knuckles on my two middle fingers holding the brush. I threw the brush, and ran to the house screaming. I made it to the kitchen slinging my hand and blood in all directions..

"What in the world is the matter now?" asked Mama.

I was incoherent by now, still screaming, still slinging blood everywhere. I finally made her understand, "A rat bit me! Mama, a dirty mean ole rat bit me!"

She grabbed a dishrag. "Well how in the world? Here, quick, put this around it," she said, and was already reaching for the peroxide. She led me to the sink and poured the peroxide across the cut knuckles. "Why isn't your dad ever here when these things happen?" She gave me a clean rag. "Here, hold this tight against your knuckles."

By now my screaming had slowed to gasping sobs. The slashes were starting to swell. "Look at this, do you think maybe my fingers are gonna fall off."

Mama looked and promised, "No they aren't. Hold the rag tight and go lie down for a while. Your dad will be home soon."

I went to sleep, but all I could see were those eyes moving closer and closer. When Daddy got home, he looked at my knuckles. "Well, Toots, I think you're gonna be OK. I killed the rat, so he won't bother you the next time you feed the rabbits."

"Daddy, I'm never gonna feed those rabbits again! I'm not even gonna go into the garage. It was awful."

"I know, but I need you to do that job. I took care of the rat. It's gone."

"But maybe the rat has a brother!"

Of course, I did continue to feed the rabbits, and there were no more rats in the garage. But for a few nights the old nightmare from long ago visited my dreams. This time, instead of Mickey, it was that feed-barrel rat who chased me across the strange machines.

I've thought about that rat bite. There were no tetanus shots, no special antibiotics, we didn't even go to a doctor. With peroxide and Daddy's magic potion salve, the swelling went down in a few days and I was fine. I guess any poison from the rat was shaken out with all the blood I splattered all over Mama's kitchen.

Toward the end of every school year, Saint Louis held an all-school open house. The teachers and kids in all grades worked for days. Miles of string crisscrossed the blackboards so that Moms and Dads and friends could admire all the hard work we'd done.

We diagrammed sentences for English, worked out multiplication and division tables for arithmetic, got finger cramps getting the ovals and push-pulls just right to show off our Spencerian penmanship, drew and colored maps for geography, built shoebox dioramas for history and the art pictures were truly masterpieces.

High school shop classes built shelves, birdhouses and tables and the home economics classes sewed aprons and dresses and baked all the cookies for refreshments. The science classes built volcanoes and many other displays. Not to be outdone, the business class typed up art pictures of presidents and birds and flowers. It was a combined visit-your-child's teacher and social occasion. The evening ended with everyone gathered in the auditorium for a band concert, singing and refreshments.

One year the open house was a big bust. The two eighth grades put their work together and had some outstanding displays—especially the one for the great run for Oklahoma. I was sure it was the best eighth grade display ever done. Our construction paper butterflies and Japanese lanterns added just the right touch. Daddy was working evenings, but I couldn't wait for Mama to see all that we had done.

But as the time for people to come passed, the student greeters had little to do. We wondered where everyone could be. The people who were there stood around in small groups and talked in whispers. Something was wrong, very wrong!

When Mama came, I asked her, "What's the matter? Where is everyone anyway? And why are these guys so quiet?"

At first Mama "hem-hawed" around a little; then she said, "There's word that an escaped prisoner killed some people up by Salt Creek. They say he's headed this way."

"Where did you hear this?" I wondered.

"Everyone's talking about it." She looked worried. "I think they may cancel the open house."

The people were so nervous, and the rumors spread. "He's hiding in the fields just north of the school. He escaped from the asylum at Norman. He's a white man. He's a black man. He's an Indian. He's kidnapped someone as a hostage. They don't even know how many he's killed."

The frightened people huddled together. No one looked at the displays. No one ate the cookies. No one visited with the teachers. Finally the Superintendent went through the building with the word that the school was closing. Everyone went home.

After we reached home, Mama said, "Keep the car doors locked. We are staying in the car till your Dad gets home at midnight."

"But, Mama . . ."

"Shut up! Don't you say a word! We are not going into that house. There's no tellin' who might be in there waiting for us." As she locked the car doors, we knew Mama was really scared.

June and I did just what Mama said. We sat in the car without saying a word till Daddy came home. He was surprised to see us and wondered what had happened. After Mama told him, he said hadn't heard a thing at the plant. He laughed and said, "O.K. Thelm', just wait here. I'll go clear out the ghosts."

"Alright, smart aleck, but you'd better take a rake or something."

Daddy went in and in a few minutes came back with the all clear. Mama still took a peek under her bed when we went in.

The next day the word came on the radio. A man HAD escaped from jail over in Seminole county. He'd never been close to our town and was captured miles away. I never knew if he had killed anyone or not.

As we took down all the displays and ate the left-over cookies, we all tried to forget the unreasonable fear that had paralyzed our community. I wondered, "Why were we all so afraid?"

Nicknames were quite common on the leases and I earned mine about this time. Groups of boys and girls would gather at Macs—a local drug store—for Cokes. For only a nickel or two, we'd sit in the booths and spend an hour talking, laughing, having fun.

At one of these gatherings Razz Hilton said, "Watch this." He tore the end off a paper straw, squeezed it and blew through it. A whistling sound came out. Soon all the other kids were trying it. All were successful with their straw whistles—all except me. I tried and tried, but the only sound I could make was a feeble "Putt" (rhymes with mutt). "Oh, shoot,"

I complained. "What's wrong with me? How come my straw says only, 'Putt'?" Everyone laughed and said, "Way to go, Putt."

The next day at school, Razz yelled across the yard, "Hey, Putt, how's your straw whistlin' going today?"

I ignored the name for awhile, but knew it wasn't going away. To tell the truth, it was better than "Mildred Louise." Even to this very day, I'm still "Putt" to all those lease friends. I never did get the straw to whistle and it's too late to try now. I don't think it would work with these modern plastic straws.

And still the war went on. Even with gas rationing and tires wearing thin, we still managed to get to Maud to the picture show about once a week; but the Saint Louis store owners decided we could use more. Once a week around dusk on a summer's evening, they would show a movie on the side of a building. Most of us sat on blankets on the ground; but there were a few chairs for the "older folks."

After the show, Jim Richmond would offer, "Hey, Putt, I could give you a ride on my bike out to your house if you want to." It was better than walking the couple of miles, so I'd say "OK, let's go," and climb on the handle bars.

But often, Pat Curtin came along on Old Red, and he'd laugh, "Hey, Putt, want a real ride?" It seemed to me that a horse's bare back was a lot more comfortable than bike handle bars, so I would gladly accept, leaving poor Jim wondering about fickle girls. This scene replayed many times till peace ended the outdoor movies.

Stamp day came around once a week at school. The savings stamps could be exchanged for War Bonds and this was our contribution to the war effort. Daddy said, "If you earn your own money, then when you exchange the stamps for a War Bond it will be really yours."

"OK. But how am I gonna earn any money?"

"Our tomatoes have lots of worms. How about a penny for every tomato worm you can pick off the vines?"

That sounded pretty good. Stamps were only a dime, so ten worms could buy a stamp. For awhile this worked, and I saved my pennies till school started. I was able to buy three stamps. But after school started, tomato season was over.

One October day Mama said, "How would like to make a little money this weekend?"

"Well, sure. What do I have to do?" Making money always sounded good.

"They're pickin' cotton over the other side of Ray City and need pickers. I heard they're paying a penny a pound if it's picked clean."

A penny for a little ole pound, huh? Gosh, I could probably make enough to buy a few stamps and have a little left over. Sounded good to me! All week I hoped it wouldn't rain on Saturday.

It didn't, and just after sun-up I climbed on my bicycle and headed for the cotton field. It was about four miles, but there were a few hills to climb, so it took me a while. Some pickers were already halfway down the rows when I got there.

After parking my bike, I went over to the man at the truck. "You lookin' for a job, little Missy?"

Little Missy, huh? Well I'll show him. "Yeah, where do I start?"

He gave me a sack more than twice as long as me. "You can work that row," he said as he pointed to a long, long row of plants filled with snowy cotton bolls. "Just put the bag over your shoulder and start pickin'. Where's your gloves?"

"I don't have any, but I'll be OK."

I looked around at the other pickers, threw the bag over my shoulder, and bent down over the first plant. "This can't be that hard. Just reach inside the boll and pull out the cotton." I reached into the first boll. "Ow, that hurt!" I looked at my scratched finger. The bolls didn't give up their white treasure easily. Now I knew why the guy had asked about gloves.

By the time our shadows had shrunk to nothing, I was no longer walking. I was crawling down the row and the bag was growing very heavy. I was glad when the lunch whistle blew.

I left the bag and went to my bicycle where my lunch was waiting. I ate the sandwich and drank the luke-warm pop. Too soon, it was time to go back to the field.

Because I had to ride my bike home, I quit a little before the others. I dragged my bag to the truck, expecting it to weigh at least a hundred pounds.

"Um—could be cleaner," the man said, "but I guess it will do. He put the bag on the scales, then counted 39 cents into my slightly bloody fingers.

"Is that all?" I couldn't believe it.

"I'm afraid so. Next week we're pullin' bolls. Maybe you'd do better at that. Come try if you want to."

"Maybe," I said. I put the 39 cents into my pocket. I was hot and tired and disappointed tears rolled down my dirty face as I rode home. There wasn't enough to buy even four saving stamps.

The burning merthiolate Mama put on my fingers brought new tears. I could hardly believe it when she said, "You know, you don't have to go back next week if you don't want to."

"But Mama, the man said next Saturday I could pull bolls and that would be easier. I'll betcha' I can do better doing that."

"Whatever you want," Mama said.

By the next Saturday, the fingers were better, the muscles were quiet again, the sun was shining and I pedaled off to the cotton field.

"Well, little Missy," the man smiled a little. "I see you're back again. Pull off just the bolls, no leaves." He handed me that same ole long sack.

"I know I can do this!" Pulling bolls was easier, but before long I still had some scratches on my fingers. (I had tried gloves. but I couldn't pull off the bolls.) I felt good when I couldn't pull my sack and the day was only half gone. That meant I'd picked a lot. After lunch, I started again with an empty sack.

By day's end I weighed in with a total 96 pounds. I could hardly stand still waiting for him to count the money into my hand, and he did—48 cents! "Wait a minute, only 48 cents? I had 96 pounds. Shouldn't I get 96 cents?"

"Well no, little Missy. For bolls, it takes two pounds to get a penny."

"You never told me that!" I muttered, then I stomped away. The ride home took forever.

Mama listened to my story, then she said "I'll give you three cents and then you'll have enough to buy nine stamps." She didn't mention going to the cotton field again.

As for me, my cotton pickin' days were over. I left pickin' cotton to the cotton pickers, but I looked at those workers through different eyes. It was a tough job!

Easter is a day of miracles. Easter Sunday, 1943, a miracle came to Cherry Hill. The Cross twins arrived! Mama Grace was well past 40 and her pregnancy had been a tough one. (I knew this only because I heard Mama say so.)

Everyone in the camp breathed a prayer of thanks when the news flew from neighbor to neighbor. "Can you believe it? Grace had TWINS!) As one so "tactfully" put it, "Land sakes, I thought she was just big. I had no idea it would be twins." I'm sure six-year-old Pauline felt left out with all the commotion over the babies. I remembered how I felt when June came along.

A couple of days after my eighth grade graduation, Grace and Virgil asked me to come to their house. After a little talk, Virgil said, "We'd like for you to help us with the twins this summer." Grace joined in, "You'll do other things too, but it's mostly with the babies that I need help. We've already talked to your Mom and Dad and it's OK with them."

"But, Miz Cross, I don't know nothin 'bout takin care of babies."

"Now it's time you called me Grace, and I know you'll do just fine. You'll learn what tending babies is all about."

And I did! Not only about tending babies, but also about cleaning house, and cooking a little. Grace's daily laid-back philosophy came as a bonus. How many times in later life did I go back to that summer to draw on all that I had learned.

Five and a-half days a week for three months, I would ride my bike or walk down to the Crosses. I usually got there just before eight and met Virgil walking across the road to the Sinclair plant. Grace would be just finishing breakfast, and I would sit with her for a little chat and a cup of cocoa while she finished her coffee. She told great stories about when she was a girl. Then the day would begin.

I helped bathe and dress Joe and Joan. I changed diapers, washed diapers, hung diapers out on the line to dry, brought them in and folded them. We kept diapers in all rooms to save steps when changing was necessary.

I helped cook dinner and had certain chores on certain days for housecleaning. I especially remember Thursdays when I would wash the red dust off all the windowsills. Since Crosses lived in one of the bigger company houses, there were lots of windows.

Except for washing clothes which we did every day, I think Grace went by the set of embroidered tea towels which spelled out which chore was to be done on which day. Sometimes there were extra things not on the tea towels like picking and snapping peas or beans for canning.

The bonus part of my job came after lunch. After the dishes were done and the babies were changed, Grace would say, "Come on, Mil, get in this big, ole comfy rocker. It's nap time—for these little 'codgers' and me."

After I sat down, she would put Joe on one overstuffed arm of the rocker and Joan on the other. They seemed to know what was coming and settled right into my arms. "See you later," said Grace as she headed for the bedroom and her own afternoon nap.

For the next hour, I rocked the babies and sang an endless tale of "Shortnin Bread." Sometimes I might switch to "Oh, Susanna" or "Comin' Round The Mountain," but they seemed to like "Shortnin Bread" best. After Grace's nap, she would take the twins and my work day was over.

All this for $3.00 per week. It was a fortune to me. I saved some of the money to buy savings stamps when school started again, but Daddy said a person should have a little of the money earned to spend. I found plenty of things to buy.

Now I know that no amount of money could ever pay for what I learned that summer. Later as I rocked my own babies to the tune of "Shortnin Bread," I felt such thankfulness for that interlude with Grace and those little "codgers."

Dora Carlton, the telephone lady, ran the Southwestern Bell telephone office in a double room at the front of her house. She lived in the back part. High school girls worked as part-time operators and in my sophomore year, she chose me.

The switchboard was a mechanical monster with jack wires that fit into little holes. There were not more than a hundred telephones in all of Saint Louis and Cherry Hill put together. Besides the private numbers, there were four party lines. That was a little tricky, to call involved a series of long and short rings which sounded in every house on the line, and any one could, and often did, listen in on the calls. (The Murphy phone, after we got one, was 1607F12—one long and two short rings.)

Long distance calls were written down in the office, then passed on to the Shawnee operator, who made the final connection. Sounds a little complicated, but really wasn't. Everything started with a courteous "Number please?"

For the next two years, I knew almost everything that happened in Saint Louis. Dora had said, "I know you'll listen to some of the conversations. Just remember, you never tell what you hear in this office." And, usually, I didn't.

The pay was $1.00 per day from 8 to 4. I think it increased to $1.25 per day before I finished. I worked on Saturdays and Sundays and some occasional nights when I would sleep on the couch in the office. Days were best because dinner included Dora's famous potato salad, the best in Pottawatomie County.

This job really made a difference in my life, then and later. At East Central State College, I worked in the cafeteria the first semester. (This was OK with me. I served coffee at the evening meal and got to know nearly everyone in the school, including those Tiger football heroes.)

Second semester, I worked at the dorm switchboard. The next year, when a switchboard job opened up in the President's office, I was lucky enough to work there the rest of my college days. The pay was $40 per month; room and board was $38 per month, so I had $2 left over for myself. And all because of Dora, the telephone lady.

And still, the war went on. In the summer of '44, Daddy surprised me. "Toots, how would you like to go to Illinois for a visit? It's been a long time."

"Sure, when do we leave?"

"We can't all go right now because our tires are no good and there's no gas, but Mama and I thought you could take the bus. You can ride up to Tulsa with Hatchells, so you'll have only the one change in St. Louis, Missouri."

I thought about what he said: I hadn't seen my folks in a long time and I knew the Marshall fair would be going on. I would be gone on my birthday and I would miss the Ada Rodeo. Still, my birthday would happen no matter where I was, and there would be other rodeos.

"OK. I guess I'd better get packed. No tellin' when I'll have another chance like this."

In less than a week, the Hatchells were ready to go. Daddy said, "Have a good time." Mama said, "You have a three-hour layover in St. Louis. It's a big place, but the bus driver will help you. Pay attention to him."

What a mistake that advice turned out to be!

The ride through the Ozarks wasn't one bit shorter than that first one. It was still dark when we turned into the bus garage in St. Louis. The driver told me, "You have a long wait here so just stay on the bus. I'll be back later to help you make your connection."

He left. There wasn't much light in the garage. I wiggled around to see if I could get more comfortable. Maybe I could read my book for awhile. I must have gone to sleep because the next thing I knew, the driver was shaking my arm.

"Better wake up now. Your bus will be in pretty soon. You'll want to be ready." He sat down on the edge of the seat across the aisle.

I put my book in my bag, checked to see if my money was still there, and took out a Mr. Goodbar that Mama said would tide me over. The driver watched me eat my candy and I began to fidget under his stare.

I was even more uneasy as he leaned toward me and said, "You know, for a little girl, you're pretty well developed."

I shoved the rest of the candy bar into my mouth and scooted farther away on the seat.

"Come on," he said softly, "why don't you open your shirt and let me have a look at you?"

My thoughts were racing. "What's the matter with this guy? Is he crazy? What kind of bus driver says stuff like this? Gosh, Mama and Daddy wouldn't like this at all." I sat very still.

He reached his hand across the aisle. "Come on. Let's have a little feel. It will be OK."

That did it. "No! Get away from me! Are you crazy? Get away right now or I'm gonna scream as loud as I can!"

I opened my mouth, but he pulled his hand back. His eyes went cold. "No, you don't have to do that. Get your stuff. I'll take you to your bus. Remember, whatever you do, this is our secret. Don't say a word to anyone about this—not a soul—or you'll be sorry."

He didn't touch me again or say anything else. He got off the bus and when I looked out, he was standing there holding my suitcase.

It was lighter in the garage now, still I wondered, "Should I follow him? But what else can I do?" As I climbed down the steps, I could see another bus down the way with a driver beside it. Just before we reached it, the hateful man turned to me and said, "Remember, not one word!"

The new driver took my suitcase, smiled and said, "Hi there, climb aboard. We're pulling out soon and should be to Marshall by dinnertime."

For some reason, I felt like I'd done something bad, but what? Had I disgraced the family? By the time I reached Marshall, I'd managed to tuck the whole thing into a little box in the back of my mind. I slammed the lid tight.

At Marshall, I found that many of my cousins had "grown up" in the years I'd been gone—especially Maurice. He seemed so shy and it took awhile for us to pick up our old way of chattering. But, before long, it was "vacation time as usual." The fair was as much fun as I remembered with rides, games and cotton candy.

Of course, farms never change, this time I made it for hay baling—a hot, itchy job. After many family get-togethers, six weeks later, I boarded another bus and headed back to Oklahoma. This time there were no problems, but I was happy to be in my own bed that first night home with the plant chugging the same old familiar lullaby, "You're home and you're safe now."

I never told anyone about what happened on that bus. Sometimes I would open the lid of that mind box just a little. I would peek inside and wonder why I felt guilty, "What happened? Why? Was it my fault? What did I do wrong?"

Life continued to change for me and everyone on the leases. Although my mama didn't go, several Moms became "Rosie Riveters" and carpooled the 60 miles to Tinker Field to build fighters and bombers. This opened up a whole new work force, which would never again be ignored by this country's industries.

With the absence of Moms and shift-working Dads, dinner-time habits on the lease changed dramatically. The camp worked out a plan so that no child was left alone for long.

Gradually the boys left town—some even before graduation. They returned in their spiffy uniforms for a short visit, before leaving again for places with names we could barely pronounce or find on the maps. Everyone waited anxiously for the tiny V-mail letters. I often wondered what words were hiding under the black marks of the censor's pen.

Three years into the war, the most dreaded of all telegrams came to the camp. Billy Wood's plane had gone down in the Pacific with no rescue. The entire camp gathered around Mode and Marie and their boys. It seemed we all had lost him and we all shared the family's grief. That very day I decided, "There is no good part to war. The parades and fancy posters are just to fool us. There must be a better way for people to live together."

Suddenly, one day in August, 1945, the war ended as quickly as it began. We looked at pictures of the mushroom clouds over Nagasaki and Hiroshima and didn't have a clue about what had been turned loose on the world. We just knew the "war to end all wars" was OVER! It was a time of great thanksgiving!

During the next two years, our country settled into a post-war mode. It was a good time in my life; I grew from a wide-eyed elementary child to a "wise" teenager. At least, I thought so.

The last two years of high school passed like a meteor crossing the sky. Our activities still centered around school, church and home. We had box suppers and cake walks, plays and talent shows, junior and senior banquets and, of course, basketball and football games.

It was because of an assembly program that my singing career ended. Frog Sullivan had borrowed my guitar. He and Sam Davis needed to practice their Boll Weevil song for a program. Unfortunately, while he had the guitar, Frog's house burned down. All that was left of the guitar was the frets and strings. I never did get another one; I never became a star. Oh, well!

When I turned 16, after the "don't disgrace the family" talk, Mama and Daddy agreed that I could have real dates. I was ready! And Bill was my choice. We went steady (the goal for every junior and senior girl) off and on for the next couple of years.

But there was a big problem at my house. Remember June? She couldn't understand why I could date at 16 and 17 years of age, and she couldn't at 9 and 10. She whined about the unfairness of this, and regularly threw dramatic fits.

As payback for all this "unfairness" she made my dating life miserable. I never knew when she would be hiding behind the couch as my boyfriend and I exchanged tender thoughts. She would pop out with giggles and say, "I heard that and I'm telling everybody on the bus." (Unfortunately, by now, most everyone could understand what she said.)

If she made it to answer a knock at the door before me, she had instant insults dripping off her tongue for the boyfriend waiting there.

Sometimes, if we were sitting outside in the swing on a summer's evening, she would sneak up behind us and give the swing a hard shove. It was not unheard of that I might fall out on my behind. And this was after I was in college.

The worst was when my boyfriend would bring me home from the picture show. If it wasn't too late, she would flip on the light just as we were saying a fond goodnight. Nothing cools down a kiss faster than an unexpected, glaring light.

As usual there was no help from Mama or even Daddy. Mama might say, "Now, June, you shouldn't tease your sister." But I think secretly Mama didn't really mind for her to discourage these guys.

Our group spent a lot of time dancing to Glenn Miller, Benny Goodman, and other "big band" performers. I still have some of old 78's on the shelf. We met at each other's houses to practice our fancy steps.

One evening a bunch of us were at my house and Mama called out as she left to go visit a neighbor, "Don't forget to roll up my new rug if you're gonna dance." That didn't take long and the jitterbugging began.

Later, before the kids left, we put the rug back. There seemed to be a problem—lumps were everywhere under the rug. "Did that look like that before?" someone asked. "Don't think so," was the reply.

"Guess what! I think we should have rolled up the pad. Guess we'd better go."

Everyone left me to face Mama alone. I tried to think of what to tell her. What a surprise when she didn't blow up the way I expected. Instead she said, "We'll have to roll the rug back and you can get rid of those lumps."

Sometimes Mama really surprised me. I did learn one thing, "If you're gonna dance at home, get down to the bare floor."

For me, swimming was even better than dancing. It gave such a feeling of freedom. Around the age of 10, Daddy said, "Toots, I think it's time you learned to swim. What do you think? We are going down to the Sulphur Park this weekend."

"Sounds good to me." I had always liked the water. It took a while to go from a flutter-kick dog paddle to a reasonable free-style stroke. Four semesters of college swimming helped a lot.

On the leases we swam anyplace we could find water—cool gravel pits; hot, red-dirt cow pasture ponds, creeks and rivers. Surely it was only guardian angels kept us from drowning.

After Seminole built a pool and some of us learned to drive, it became our favorite summertime hang out. The required "pig sandwich" at the Pig Stand after the swim, meant we'd have to make excuses for not being hungry at suppertime.

It was at the Seminole pool that I caught my first glimpse of the new Methodist preacher's son. I'd heard rumors that there was a pretty "neat" new guy in town. The rumors were right, he was neat. As time passed, that glimpse proved to be very significant.

"The Snowstorm" during the winter of '46 was one to be remembered. Anything over half an inch of snow in central Oklahoma created problems, this was the granddaddy of all snowstorms. A few days after Christmas, the snow began to fall, and fell steadily for the next three days till something close to a foot was piled up.

Nothing moved! The sun and rising temperatures were about the only snow removal equipment available. Luckily for me, I was in town when it started and stayed there for the next four days. On the second day, Mr. Elliott took grocery orders at the camp and came to town in a big company truck.

He looked me up and asked me if I wanted to go out to Cherry Hill. "Are you crazy/" I thought, "and miss all the parties?" What I said was, "Naw, thanks anyway. Tell Mama I'll be home in a couple of days."

"Haramph!" was Mr. Elliott's reply. "You can tell her yourself when the phones start working."

We skated on Hilton's pond. No ice skates, but shoes worked pretty well. The boys went rabbit hunting, cleaned the rabbits and took them to Sam's Mom. My mama made it to town by then and she and Mrs. Davis and Mrs. Waller fried the rabbits and made biscuits and gravy. Mrs. Davis took cans of peaches off their grocery shelves, and we kids had a feast fit for the gods.

Too soon the New Year came, and we began our final semester of high school.

As graduation day came closer, we kept having the "spur-of-the-moment" get-togethers. Our Moms were always ready to throw together some potato salad with the trimmings to add to our "after-church" picnics. It was kind of like our parents were thinking, "This only happens only once, so go for it. Enjoy these days." And we did.

I knew I had to write a speech for the night of graduation. One day I realized I didn't have much time, so I went outside with a pencil and paper. I really needed a tree to sit in for proper thinking, but a quilt in the shade had to do.

I looked back over the years spent at Cherry Hill and Saint Louis. Not every memory was a good one, but most of them were and I realized how blest we'd been. I put some words down, I knew my speech teacher, Mr. Mason, would probably tear it apart, but this was the best I could do.

Not long ago I found the speech again. Two of the thoughts I shared at that time were: "The spirit of Saint Louis High will ever be a force for good in our lives. The love of her we will ever hold in our hearts." That pretty much still says it for me.

The speech teacher kept telling me, "You've got to practice. It's a good speech, but you will embarrass yourself and everyone else if you stammer through it."

On the afternoon of the last practice, most of the class was going swimming. How could I miss that? Besides I'd practiced a lot. I knew that speech forward and backward. I skipped practice and went swimming.

That night as the graduates were lining up to go into the auditorium, Mr. Mason came down the hall. No surprise, he was hopping mad. "I'll be fine. I know the speech." Just to be sure, I gave a copy to a friend sitting in the front row to cue me in a pinch.

Mama and Daddy, relatives from Illinois and friends from Seminole were all in the audience ready to be proud. When time for the speech came, I walked to the microphone with confidence, gave a big smile and began.

"This is going well," I thought. All of a sudden, I went totally blank. There was no way I was ever gonna remember the next word. It was very quiet. I looked at my friend for my cue. He was giving it but, as always, I wasn't wearing my glasses, so I couldn't see him very well. I couldn't hear him either. I stepped out from behind the podium, leaned over the edge of the stage and said, "I can't hear you."

He gave me the next words in a louder voice. I stepped back behind the podium and finished the speech in a blaze of glory. That wasn't the only blaze. The faces of my parents, relatives, and friends were also glowing.

As I left the stage, there was applause, mostly in sympathy for my parents, I think.

I went down the steps to my seat and glanced at Mr. Mason. He was snarling, "I told you so." He didn't like for his speech students to make mistakes.

"Oh, well," I thought, "Nothing's gonna ruin this night," and it didn't. I had just finished 12 years of a wonderful time in my life.

After graduation, Daddy said there was a surprise for me. "Toots, your Mama and I thought you might like to play a little this summer before you start at East Central. How would you like to go to Oregon (Illinois) Bible College for a few weeks?"

This was a surprise. They had already given me a cedar chest for graduation. Mama said it was a "hope chest" and I could fill it up with things for my wedding. "Gosh, Mama, I hardly have a boy friend right now. I don't see a wedding anytime soon."

There was no reason not to go. "Sure, why not? When do I leave?"

The next week I found myself on a Greyhound headed north. I had a couple of bad thoughts of that "other" trip, but I reminded myself, "I'm all grown up now and can certainly handle things a little better."

The summer session of the Bible College was more like a camp experience than a college. We lived in a dorm, made our own beds, kept our rooms clean and washed our own dishes. About 30 kids from all over the country and Canada were attending. Classes were held mornings and afternoons, with preaching and gospel singing at night.

We played basketball and softball and swam a lot. We had fun, but for me, it was a time of spiritual growth. In the "flurry" of a Senior year in high school, I'd gotten a little off track in the direction of my Christian life. This was a renewal time, and I found my faith was still a part of me and it grew stronger than ever. (I wondered if Daddy had something like this in mind when he chose this gift.)

After goodbyes from new friends, I took my first train ride to spend a week with Aunt Stella in Chicago. Everyday was a different treat—museums, art galleries, downtown Chicago for a little shopping and a lot of looking, and the Lake Michigan shoreway. Aunt Stella saved the best for last. We went to the theater where Peggy Lee was performing. The show was opened by the comic pianist, Victor Borge. It was like a dream come true for me.

Aunt Martha came to Chicago to get me. When we reached Marshall, Mama and Daddy were already there. After our vacation, we returned to Oklahoma. I was in for another surprise.

While I was gone, Mama and Daddy bought a house. Actually we had lived in the house for a few months before we moved to Texas, but this time they bought it. Mama was so proud. She would say, "This is my first real home and, to think, it was only $60." I know that sounds like an awful place, but actually, it was better than most boomshacks. There were nice cabinets in the kitchen and a closed-in back porch for Mama's washing machine. The room for June and me had been built on, with a bathroom.

The thing I liked best was the front yard. A porch swing was suspended between two big trees. It was always shaded, and at night was a perfect place to spend a little time with a boyfriend, especially the preacher's son. (Beware of little sisters!)

September came and I began life at East Central. It was all I could hope for. I discovered the fascination of a foreign language, Latin. Some people thought I was crazy taking Latin, but I loved the orderliness of the language. It was only by chance that my second teaching job happened because the school needed a Latin teacher.

From the beginning, I knew that I DID want to be a teacher and I wanted to get through college in three years. I went summer terms, August terms, and took a couple of correspondence classes and made my goal. I graduated in July, 1950, with a major in business and minors in English and Latin.

Daddy said, "A business major is a good idea. If you don't like teaching, you can always work in an office."

I was busy at school, but had a good time, too. The cafeteria was in the girls' dorm, so the boys were there often. There was dancing and pinochle games in the huge living room. It's rumored that some "spooning" went on in the rose garden behind the dorm. Of course, I wouldn't know anything about that.

Pinochle was almost my downfall during my sophomore year. I liked to play and I would often cut classes to join the game. Some of my grades were in jeopardy. In those days, colleges kept in close contact with parents, so after Daddy's little talk with me, I "rethunk" my priorities and the value of pinochle. Grades improved dramatically.

A radio news bulletin one hot day barely caught my attention as I hurried across the dorm living room. I was just starting my last term at East Central. "President Truman is calling this a police action, as he sends U. S. troops into South Korea."

I hesitated. "What does that mean, a police action?" I wondered. "Must not be too much." Little did I know that day, June 25, 1950, that the "police action" would change my life completely in the months ahead.

My first teaching job began that fall at Centerview, a small consolidated school south of Prague. My duties included five business classes, one English class, library supervisor, Junior Class advisor, director of the Junior Class play, and, in the second year, girls' basketball coach. I lived on the school grounds in a small duplex, shared with another teacher.

For this, I received $2,400 a year, and if the truth be told, I probably should have paid them for all the things I learned that first year. I had an understanding superintendent, Mr. Spencer, who let me learn from my mistakes as long as it didn't hurt the kids.

My students were about one-third Polish ancestry, one-third Sac and Fox Indian, and one third farm kids. Since I had just turned 21 years old when I started, some of the students were almost as old as I was. Surprisingly they were relatively patient with me. Before the year was over, I believe we came to like and respect each other. I discovered I loved teaching and had made the right career choice.

It was at Centerview that I met my Sac and Fox family, the Rices. They took me to their hearts and shared with me many wondrous things of their Native American culture.

Remember the new Methodist preacher's son? We sort of got together that first Christmas holiday when we were both home from college after my high school graduation. As time passed, with a few off and on times, we began to date rather seriously. By the fall of my first teaching year, he was the only guy in my life. Then Uncle Sam decided that "police action" was going to need more troops. James was drafted and went to Fort Sill and then to Camp Chaffee, in Arkansas where he was stationed for several months.

I continued to teach at Centerview. James called me late in January, 1952, and said he was coming to Saint Louis for the weekend and could I meet him there. I thought this was a little strange, he'd just been home for the Christmas holidays.

Late that Sunday night we were talking, when out of the blue, he surprised me with, "I guess I'll be gone for awhile. They're sending me to Korea."

My first thought was, "This 'police action' is sounding a lot like a war to me."

"Um, when do you have to go?"

"In a couple of weeks; I have to go back to Camp Chaffee on Monday to get everything squared away. I'll be back on Wednesday. I was wondering if maybe we could get married before I go?"

That left me speechless. Of course I'd thought about it, but that first surprise didn't compare to this one. Still I had an answer ready and didn't hesitate.. "Sure! When, do you think?"

"I thought maybe next Sunday, if Dad can come down and do it." The Dennises had moved to another town a couple of years before.

"OK. Sure! We'll have a lot to do this week. I have to be at school because the girls are playing in the county basketball tournament, and we're having semester exams. Mother will have to make my dress." Luckily, I had some wedding dress material in my hope chest.

"I'll talk to your Dad in the morning. I guess we'd better get some sleep now."

"Yeah, I guess." I knew I'd sleep very little the rest of THAT night! As I crawled into bed with June, I hardly noticed that she immediately scooted over to my side. Thoughts chased each other across my mind.

I doubt James slept much either, especially since he was sleeping with Daddy.

The next morning, after much hesitation, James asked Daddy about the wedding. He told him he was headed for Korea in a couple of weeks. My parents were surprised, I guess, but agreed to pull everything together.

The next morning I called Bonnie, my ole college roommate. "Think you could come down next Sunday? Uh, James and I are getting married." First a long pause, then she sputtered, "Are you kidding? I mean, sure, you know. I'll be there!" And just as we'd always planned, she was there to get me to the church almost on time.

With the help of just about every one in the camp, we had a beautiful formal wedding the next Sunday afternoon. Mother made the dresses for June and me. Daddy took care of the cake and got the invitations in a day. Someone addressed them. Mrs. Waller took over the reception. Late on Saturday night before the wedding, my grandmother and other relatives arrived from Illinois. Unfortunately, the usher couldn't make it from the San Antonio Air Force Base, but David our brother-in-law filled in.

Mr. Spencer gave me three days off from school, and we had a brief honeymoon. James left from Will Rogers Airport 13 days later. As I watched the lights of the plane disappear into the night sky, I thanked God for our happiness, and asked that He might bless us and keep my husband safe until we could be together again.

I kept busy at school and haunted the mail box, watching for letters with the APO number in the return. After school was out, I decided to return to East Central and take some graduate courses. I went back to work at the switchboard, but almost immediately was offered a secretarial job at the college. I was seriously considering it. If I worked at East Central, James could continue his college education at the college after he came home from Korea.

On Memorial Day, the office was open and I was working. But I had a feeling I really needed to go home and talk to Daddy about the job offer. Roberta said, "Sure, go ahead. We're not busy. I'll see you Monday."

"OK. I'll just leave right now. If I hurry, I should get to see him before he goes to work. I know he's on the evening shift."

I got home about 3:15. Daddy was still at home; he'd been talking with Joyce Dunagun about taking her wedding pictures. He was surprised to see me, "What are you doing here? I thought you were working today."

"Something has come up. Daddy, can we talk before you go to work?"

"Sure, Toots, what is it?"

"Well, East Central has made me a job offer. It isn't teaching and I know that's what you would want me to do; it's a secretarial job. I figured if I took it, James could finish his degree there. Then I could always go back to teaching, 'cause you know, I really like it."

We talked for awhile and time was getting short. "I'll take you to work. Mama can bring your lunch later. June, you want to ride over with us?"

We got into the car, and I took him the half-mile to the plant. We sat in front for a little bit. "Take a look at my strawberry preserves I made this week while your Mom was gone," he said. "Take a couple of jars back to school with you."

Then, as he started to get out, he smiled and reassured me, "Don't worry about this, Toots. We'll talk some more when I get home at midnight. You don't have to decide right now. You know it's gonna be OK."

He shut the car door, turned and waved to us before he disappeared around a building.

Mama's company had left and later she went in to fix Daddy's lunch. She asked us if we wanted something, but we decided we would go to Pearson Café for sandwiches later. When she got back from the plant, she said, "That's funny, Lucian usually comes down to the gate to get his lunch. Maybe they're having some trouble over there."

We were ready to leave, when we heard three sharp whistles coming from the plant. "I told you they were having trouble," Mama said. We went outside, and could see a couple of men running toward the buildings.

As we watched, we saw a car leave, and as it neared our house, Virgil Cross pulled in. "Y'all better come with me. We have a problem at the plant."

When we got there, we got out and someone started talking to Mama. Virgil put his arm around me and said, "You're gonna have to be strong. Your dad is gone. We aren't gonna tell your Mama yet."

I just looked at him. "No, you're wrong. He can't be dead, Virgil. We didn't finish talking. He's coming home at midnight to help me decide what to do. He told me he would."

But Virgil was right. I was wrong. We followed the ambulance to the Seminole hospital. Before long, a doctor came into the waiting room and told Mama. The nightmare began.

When we got home around midnight, the house was full of people. Food filled the kitchen. Mama went from person to person with a dazed look. People looked to me for answers to their questions. Poor June must have been lost, but I honestly can't remember what was happening with her.

The next day I called James' dad to see if he could come to preach the Sunday service for the Saint Louis funeral. "We will use the Baptist Church because it has more room." I asked the Red Cross to send a telegram to James, but the person on the phone said, "He can't come home, so you take care of it." Finally, I sat down and wrote him a letter. It was ten days later that he even knew my Daddy was gone.

Saturday night my Sac and Fox family came from Centerview. As we stood together by the swing, Papa Rice prayed to the Great Father, and we all drank water to help wash our grief away.

I remember very little about the Sunday service, except that the church was full. Many friends stood up in the back. After people said their "goodbyes," Daddy was taken to Seminole to the train for his trip home to Illinois.

We left a little later. Mama rode with Grace and Virgil and the twins. I drove my car, with my Indian sister, Jessie Rice's help and June and Pauline rode with us.

In Illinois, both Mama and Daddy's family filled the funeral home for the wake. It was like a family reunion with lots of talk and laughter. I wanted to scream at them, "Just shut up. This is not a happy time. Don't you know my Daddy is DEAD?"

As usual, Jessie seemed to sense how I felt. She came over, took my hand and whispered softly, "Come on, Murph, let's take a walk." As we moved along under the trees, we didn't say anything, but gradually, my soul found a quiet place on the hateful hot afternoon.

My experience with death was so limited. Daddy's was only the second funeral I'd ever gone to in Saint Louis. The other one was for Mr. Elliott who had died suddenly three years earlier.

The oppressive heat was like an oven as we rode the eight dusty miles to that little country cemetery in Clarksville, the little town where Daddy had been born, where his father's store had been, where I had been born. For him, I believe it was a peaceful place to be—his home. But, I also believe "home" for Daddy had always been wherever he was.

We left the next day and returned to Oklahoma. My aunts and uncles had made Mama promise she would return to Illinois to live. (June and I were not happy about this.)

I returned to East Central, but soon I found that I couldn't stay there. The Mama that I knew who had always been so strong was now devastated. She was not able to make decisions about what needed to be done and she wanted me to come home. James had finally received the letter about Daddy, and his reply gave me strength, "Honey, I'm so sorry. I should be there with you, but I know you will do what needs to be done. Remember that I love you and I will be home one day."

I was trying to deal with my own feelings. I was so angry, but at whom? At Daddy? He couldn't keep from dying. At God? I just wanted to know, "Why?" A Daddy is not supposed to die at 46. Maybe helping Mama would help me.

I quit school and went home. Mama was adamant about one thing—she was moving to Illinois. As she packed, we sorted out what needed to go with her and what could be sold. Finally, in August, everything was ready. She sold her $60 house for $600. Some high school kid bought the old green '37 Ford. June and I asked him to please take care of it.

A couple of cousins came from Illinois with a truck and loaded what was left to go. Early one morning in August, it was time to leave. I couldn't believe it was raining; it never rains in Oklahoma in August. I brushed the rain out of my eyes, the drops were suspiciously salty, and pulled out of the driveway. I knew, this time, I was truly leaving the lease behind. I never lived at Cherry Hill or on any other oil lease again.

But Cherry Hill never left my heart. Occasionally we would pass through there on the way to visit James' folks. Gradually the oil wells stopped flowing, the plant became a pump station, then less than that. All of the company houses were torn down or moved. Most of the other houses are gone. First the Saint Louis High School, then the elementary closed. It sat desolate for awhile, but now it has new life. Paul Postman, a former student, is turning the old high school into a beautiful, unique home.

The town is almost gone. Hilton's store still sits on the corner, now closed. A new post office is on the other corner, serving the couple of hundred people who live in the area.

The former students of Saint Louis have a strong alumni association and we meet once a year to relive our days together and twist the Tiger's tail a little.

EPILOGUE

After the 2004 alumni reunion, James and I returned to Saint Louis. We followed the blacktopped road from Pop City to Cherry Hill. Not much had changed since my last visit a couple of years earlier. The trees had grown taller, the scrub brush thicker. It had been a rainy spring and where the camp houses had been, the cattle stood belly-deep in Johnson grass.

We pulled into the weed-filled sandy path that led back to where Mama's $60 house had been. It's a road little used now. I stopped. "James, I'm gonna' walk back and see if I can find where the house stood."

"Go ahead. Stay as long as you like. I'll wait for you here."

As I made my way, I could see a good stand of sticker burrs and goatheads. Only one of the two trees that had supported the swing remained. I went a little further to a small sandy clearing. "This must be it," I thought.

I reached down and picked up a fistful of the red sandy dirt, then looked across the gully. A couple of the towers from the plant were still standing. It was too quiet.

As I closed my eyes, I thought, "This IS MY place. It helped make me who I am and nothing can take that away."

What was that sound? Could it be the old swing creaking in the wind? Many of the dreams I spun in that swing have come to pass; some haven't. But Daddy, as you always promised, "It really has been OK."

Almost, almost, I could hear Mama calling, "Come on home now, it's supper time."

I lifted my eyes to that matchless blue sky, and let the dirt sift between my fingers. The ever-blowing wind caught it and the small red cloud drifted away.

In that moment a thought took root in my heart, "Someday, someone will stand on this very spot and remember me. The dust of my bones will sift through their fingers to mix with this red dirt on which I stand, and my soul will soar into that endless blue sky.

On that day, another Oklahoma lease-child will enter eternity!"

About the Author

Mildred Dennis has always been a story teller. She wrote an award-winning newspaper column which appeared weekly in Illinois and Ohio for 25 years. She drew from life with her husband, her three children, her high school students, a love of nature, an enduring faith in God, and memories of growing up on the Oklahoma oil leases for her material.

Other published works include three books of meditations and numerous magazine articles. As a Methodist lay speaker, her talks centered around her faith and she has led seminars on the stresses of caregiving and grief. She especially enjoys Storytelling with children and nursing home residents.

Since retiring, she and husband James travel extensively around the U.S. She enjoys swimming, crocheting, all of outdoors, old-time gospel singing, reading, and, above all, being with family.

CPSIA information can be obtained at www.ICGtesting.com
Printed in the USA
LVOW13s0540300514

387796LV00003B/4/P